Denise,

Sophie and Ben

by

Helen Nardecchia

Best Wishes!

Helen Nardecchia

10/15/14

Sophie and Ben

Copyright 2001
by
Helen Nardecchia
ISBN 0-9700616-6-0

Word Wright International
P.O. Box 1785
Georgetown, Texas 78627

Printed in the United States of America

My love and thanks go to my husband, Bud, who is Sophie and Ben's son. Without his encouragement and help, this tribute to his parents would not have been accomplished. I also want to thank the other members of my family who were so supportive in compiling this story.

Sophie at 12 years old in Bluff Springs, Texas, 1921

Acknowledgement

Sophie Veronica Rizzo, is and always has been a vivacious, independent human being, and even at times incorrigible. However, in the last ten years, we have learned to know one another better, and I would even venture to say that we have become good friends.

This book is not a documentary of her life, but rather an account based on her life. The names of her children are authentic, but at her request, other names and places have been changed for personal reasons.

Foreword

My husband, Bud, and I lived in Chicago and raised our family there for thirty-five years before moving to Austin, Texas. Bud was born in Del Valle, and raised in Austin. His dream to retire and return to Texas, became a reality a few years back when we moved into a new home in the Jester Estates area.

Upon returning to Austin, I became friends with my now 92-year-old mother-in-law whom I really never knew very well. Sophie was the mother of six children, all fathered by Ben Nardecchia, who passed away in 1966. Bud was her second child.

There were many occasions when she and I sat in her living room, while sunshine peaked into a large plate glass window, that she would reminisce about her marriage to Ben and the difficulty of raising a family in Texas. After hearing her stories repeated over and over again, I decided to take a pad and pen along one day to document what I considered to be a very interesting life. Before going back many years to a girl of twelve years old, I would like to introduce you to Sophie as she is now.

In spite of her 92 years, she is vibrant and energetic; loves her yard and spends countless hours working the soil and planting vegetables and flowers. She takes pride in her "green thumb," and bubbles with enthusiasm when her neighbors ask the names of different plants and how she gets them to look so good.

"You never over water," she will caution. "And by all means, use compost soil."

Her petite, four-foot-ten-inch body may be a bit bent and weathered from age and the hot sun, but her spirit is fresh and exuberant.

It is Sophie's custom to work outdoors all morning, and after lunch relax in her favorite chair in the living room. Sometimes, she reads for long stretches and other times, may talk to herself, bringing back old memories and events of long ago.

When the weather isn't very good, and she is confined to the house, she will spend hours looking through old photographs. She keeps pictures of family strewn all around the coffee table at all times, so visitors can roam through them asking questions, like, "Who's this?" and "What year was that?"

She loves to talk about the past and will tell every good thing or bad, that happened to her in her lifetime. On occasions, she will pick up a picture of her parents; Nofria, her mother, who lived to be 96 years old and Salvatore, her patient, sweet father whom she loved dearly. His tragic death came much earlier than Nofria's and remembering brings tears to her eyes as she looks back over the years.

Sophie may reflect often on the trials of her life with great trepidation, but will never regret leaving the toil and drudgery of the Texas cottonfields.

Chapter 1

Salvatore and Nofria

Sophie's parents, Salvatore and Nofria Rizzo, were both born in Sicily. Salvatore was warm natured, a man of medium height and slender build. It was not until much later in life that he became stocky, even bullish looking. Nofria, was just the opposite. She was slender, appeared taller than she really was, and displayed a more serious nature.

They met and married in New York in 1905, but due to a legal matter that had to be settled in their hometown of Partenica, in the Province of Palermo, they returned to Sicily. Nofria's parents owned land in this region, and when her father died, it was decided that the land be sold.

Since her mother would be living with them in America they felt it was not necessary to keep the land. However, it was not easy to sell, and took longer than they anticipated. A wine merchant purchasing large amounts of land to cultivate vineyards finally bought it up.

It was in 1906, while they were living in Sicily, that Nofria gave birth to their first child; a daughter they named Lena. The baby was stillborn and brought a great deal of sadness to the young couple. However, one year later Nofria became pregnant again. At the end of the pregnancy, her labor was long and painful. She feared the possibility of another fatal birth, but the second child, a little girl, born September 26, 1908, was healthy and beautiful. They called her Sophie Crosifina. "Crosifina" was given to her as a second name because Nofria prayed to the crucifix hanging on the bedroom wall through the entire labor.

Nofria and Salvatore remained in Italy until 1913. Sophie was five years old when they returned to America and they settled in Monroe, Michigan, mainly because other members of Salvatore's family lived there and they were encouraged to come. Salvatore was uneducated and limited in reading and writing, but with family help and recommendations, he was able to get a job in a toy factory.

Sophie, on the other hand, was adjusting quite well in Michigan and was beginning to grow into a lovely young lady. She was petite with beautiful dark brown eyes and wavy black hair.

She loved school. She was a bright, exuberant child with unbridled energy. Her mind was sharp and she learned quickly; but sadly, at that time, it was felt education was wasted on a girl, and Nofria expected her to be more domestic. Salvatore, always her ally, would remind Nofria that she was just a little girl.

Being a normal adolescent, she objected to household chores, and longed for friendships and excitement.

"Why, I recall," she said to me as she told her story, "my grandmother pulling my hair as hard as she could because I smiled at a boy one day."

In the fall of 1920, Sophie had just turned twelve years old. She was in her room, deep into her schoolwork, when she heard her parents discussing a possible move quite far away.

She heard her mother say, "Austin, Texas? Where is that?"

They were happy in their new home, and probably would have remained in Michigan had it not been for Salvatore's health. He began to cough and have repeated illnesses. After a couple of visits to a doctor, it was realized that the chemicals and dyes used in the factory were the cause of his medical problems.

Bronchitis ran in Salvatore's family, and so the doctor suggested that he move to a warmer climate to dry up the mucus and fluids that lingered in his lungs and bronchial tubes.

After Salvatore convinced Nofria that he could not continue to work in the toy factory plans were made to move. Sophie was not happy about this development at all. She loved school. She even enjoyed walking to school in the snow, but none of this was as important as Salvatore's health, and so, he began to make arrangements for taking his family to Texas.

One day after school, her mother said, "We are in touch with some friends in Texas, Sophie. I have written a letter for your father telling them about his health, and they have said for us to come. They are sure he will find work once we get there. Your father wants to leave soon. They have sent the name of a man who may help him find a job. It is Franzoni, Mr. Franzoni."

Sophie asked, "When do we leave?" Nofria said "Couple of weeks." Moving would not be easy for Nofria. Not only were there two other children in the family besides Sophie, Angelina and Joseph, but Nofria discovered she was pregnant again.

Chapter 2

Farewell to Michigan

One month later, after much packing in small and large boxes, Sophie awoke to the sound of horses neighing out front. She quickly jumped out of bed to look out the window. There she saw a neighbor arranging his wagon with their boxes and suitcases while Angelina and Joseph, her little brother and sister were playing on the ground with a toy. Sophie dressed and went downstairs; realizing the day had come when she'd no longer have the things she loved the most.

As she entered the kitchen, Nofria looked her way and said, "Sophie, give the children some breakfast and feed yourself. We will be leaving soon. Mr. Roselli is taking us to the train station."

The wagon was packed to the brim as Salvatore and his family, including Grandma, Nofria's mother, all climbed in to begin their first step to a new life. Sophie fought back tears as she hugged her doll and waved goodbye to what would now become a memory.

The train ride from Michigan to Texas took ten days. It was long and tedious with the little children becoming antsy and bored. In spite of not knowing what lay ahead, all were happy to see the trip end.

Sophie's parents were apprehensive as they looked around. Their eyes saw a different world altogether as they stepped down from the train. It was August, and the heat struck them with a vengeance; it was unbearable. Today, we can look for relief by escaping indoors with air-conditioning, but they did not have that pleasure.

Salvatore wondered if he had made a mistake dragging his family to this forsaken, hot land, but as time went on he stopped coughing, his health improved and everyone made the necessary adjustments. Supporting his family became the problem.

He contacted Mr. Franzoni, as friends in Texas had instructed, but was terribly disappointed when he found out the type of work he would be doing. Mr. Franzoni owned cotton fields and needed cotton pickers. Square shouldered, tall and distinguished looking, Mr. Franzoni told Salvatore he had his choice of picking cotton or baling cotton. Baling cotton meant tying it into bundles and weighing it on scales. He did not like his choices.

He thought seriously about not taking this job. He had come from a cool climate and was not conditioned to working outdoors in the heat of the southwest. However, after much consideration, he realized he had no choice. Salvatore's education was so limited that there would not be many other opportunities out there for him to accept. So, he told Mr. Franzoni he would take the job, and because his reading and writing abilities were practically nil, he was assigned to picking cotton.

Mr. Franzoni informed Salvatore that he and his family

would be living in a small house in the near vicinity of the cotton fields. They had been staying with a cousin up to this time.

"Salvatore," said Mr. Franzoni. "You and your family come to my house for dinner Sunday and I will give you all the details." Salvatore accepted.

They arrived in the early afternoon and were greeted pleasantly by Mr. Franzoni and his family. Sophie was delighted to see a young girl about her age. Her name was Tina, and Sophie hoped they could become friends. In fact, Mrs. Franzoni, a lovely stout woman with curly salt and pepper hair, suggested that Sophie and Tina sit together at the dinner table so they could chat. Sophie loved this because she had never had a close friend before. Tina was very pretty, but had a complexion directly opposite of Sophie's. She was very fair with blue eyes and blonde hair.

The visit spent with Tina Franzoni is still fresh in Sophie's mind and she loves to talk about it. Tina was fun and they laughed a lot. She was excited over the fact that Tina had a camera, which was something Sophie never had at that age. In fact, most of their fun was looking through an album Tina had put together with pictures of her friends and family. Tina's mother sewed beautifully and made all her clothes, justifying the large selection she had in her closet. Sophie hoped she would see Tina again, but this did not come to pass.

On their way back to their cousin's house, Salvatore said to Nofria, "We will move into one of the houses tomorrow morning,"

Nofria hesitated a moment and then said, "I'm a little

scared!"

Salvatore said, "So am I. I moved here because of my health and to work in the cotton fields in this heat might make it worse."

Mr. Franzoni had given Salvatore a tour of the cotton fields, pointing out the houses. He wasn't impressed. The houses were small, each designed and built alike, and the fields were large, to say nothing about the hot sun. "We will try, Nofria. We will try," was all Salvatore said as they rode back to the cousin's house.

Chapter 3

We Will Make Do

The following morning, Mr. Franzoni drove Salvatore and his family to one of the houses. He stopped the buggy and got out, took a bunch of keys from his pocket and walked slowly up on the porch. Nofria watched him closely as he opened the front door. She could easily see that it was a very small house without any warmth. There were no flowers, no bushes, and not even any trees. Mr. Franzoni beckoned for them to follow, and they all reluctantly got down from the buggy. Salvatore led the pack with Grandma close behind. Sophie's mother was not excited about this new venture. She was the last to enter the house.

The entrance of the house ran right into a parlor with an arch separating two rooms, which gave the effect of an open parlor, dining-room look. The two small rooms then led into a tiny kitchen with just enough room to cook and wash dishes. In back of the kitchen was a small, screened porch that Nofria thought could be used for a sewing room. Knowing how much she loved to sew, she smiled silently to herself feeling pleasure in that thought.

To the left of the dining room were two bedrooms, with a small room in the center. The room contained a dressing table where a bowl and pitcher could be placed for bathing. A mirror could also be placed over the dressing table, if desired. But to Nofria's displeasure, there was no bathtub. There was room, however, to install one later. She hoped they would be able to afford such a luxury.

Another thing that bothered her was the stark gray paint on the walls. Much indeed would have to be done to brighten their home.

Mr. Franzoni then directed them outside where he pointed out a water pump that was located at the far end of the yard. Several feet from the pump sat a privy. Large tubs for washing clothes were placed against the house, and a clothesline was draped across the yard. He informed them that the water pump was to be shared by all the houses on the land.

Sophie could hear her mother sigh as she noticed the long walk from the pump to the wash tubs. Salvatore stayed close behind Mr. Franzoni, as they looked the house and property over. He allowed his mind to drift a minute wondering what Nofria might be thinking. He purposely avoided looking at her for fear that anger might show in her face. However, as he and Mr. Franzoni were unloading the wagon, he felt a gentle hand on his shoulder and turned to see her standing behind him. She smiled and said, "We will make do."

Chapter 4

The Storm Cloud

A few months after the family had settled into their new surroundings, Nofria awoke one morning and started her usual routine of making coffee. She had learned to love the small house, in spite of the crowded conditions and inconveniences. She had also done a tremendous amount to improve its appearance. Nothing could be done to the gray walls since Mr. Franzoni objected, but she added lots of color with curtains, bedspreads, area rugs, pillows, and whatever else looked depressing to her.

The early morning was her favorite time of the day, and in the quiet she could get a lot of sewing done. As the day wore on it would get hotter and she would only handle chores that were absolutely essential. Thus, enjoying the breeze blowing in the windows on the screened back porch, she would slip back into her past and remember pleasant memories of long ago. Like the time she and her mother traveled from Sicily to New York, and had seen America for the first time. The year was 1905.

She remembered the majestic sight of the Statue of Liberty and the tears of joy that she and her fellow passengers shared when they passed through immigration on Ellis Island. She was just a teenager then, short in statue. Not as pretty a teenager as Sophie, but attractive in the way she presented herself.

Nofria's father, August Garifo, sailed to America first to find a job and set up comfortable living arrangements for his family. He was able to find a job in a factory through friends and relatives, and saved enough money to purchase tickets for Nofria and her mother, Angela, to sail to America.

They were happy in this new land and she remembered Angela saying, "You are a young lady now, and it's time you look for a husband. It will be easier here in New York. There are a lot of handsome men." Nofria would blush. She was very shy.

Truthfully, she wasn't interested in men and had no desire to marry. That is, until she met Salvatore. He worked with August at the factory and somehow was always at their house. He loved her at once, but it took her a little longer to see his warmth and charm.

Finally, without even realizing it, Salvatore became someone with whom she wanted to share her life. They were married in the Catholic Church in 1905.

Nofria smiled to herself while on the porch, remembering the past and feeling now she had made a good choice in marrying Salvatore.

Suddenly, Nofria was brought back to reality by a sound of someone approaching on horseback. She slowly left the sewing machine and looked out the window over the sink. There was a rather attractive man in the saddle coming toward the porch. She did not recognize him and became frightened. After all, it was quite early for a visitor to call on home folks. She remained at the window a long time and watched as he trotted around the house, never leaving the saddle, just seemed to be looking over the land.

Nofria woke Salvatore and together they approached the stranger. Whether Sophie saw him from her bedroom window or not, is not clear, but it was on this particular day that Ben Nardecchia entered their lives. He was looking for work and Salvatore showed him where the Franzonis lived.

Ben rode his horse up to the front of the Franzoni home, dismounted, strolled up to the front door and knocked. Sergio opened the door hurriedly; thinking it was one of their workers and stopped. He could not believe his eyes and could only say, "Ben, Ben, is that you?"

Ben smiled and Sergio hugged him with all his strength. Ben and Sergio were close companions during their wandering days in Germany. There was great merriment that evening in the Franzoni household and Ben and Sergio talked to late in the night about old times. Mr. Franzoni knew Ben was looking for work and hired him that evening.

Sophie remembers Mr. Franzoni, his son and Ben arriving at their house one evening to ask if Sophie could help work in the cotton fields. Nofria was not eager to let Sophie go because she was so helpful in taking care of the younger children. However, the added income was needed and so she said, "I will talk it over with Salvatore and let you know. "You know, it is very hot out there and she is very young."

"I know, Nofria, but Sophie is strong. I think she can handle it. I will need an answer by tomorrow," remarked Franzoni.

During this conversation, Ben never took his eyes off Sophie, and after they left, the newly arrived young man stayed in Sophie's mind.

Salvatore agreed that Sophie should help out in the cotton fields, even though Sophie was not happy to hear this. It was early May, and he felt that by August she would change her mind. To console her, Nofria suggested that the children accompany her to a berry picking. She knew this was one of Sophie's favorite things to do. There were several farmhouses along St. Elmo Road where farmers planted blueberries. So they started out.

After picking two baskets of berries, Nofria suggested they start for home. Upon returning, she and the little ones went into the house while Sophie, feeling peaceful inside decided to stay outdoors. She found an old rope on the front porch and began to tie it into knots. After wandering off the porch into the yard, she began to jump rope, saying out loud, "A, my name is Anna, my husband's name is Albert. We come from Africa with a ship load of apples."

Unconsciously, she looked up into the sky, then stopped suddenly. There was a large, black mass coming from the west toward her. At first, she thought it was a huge screen of smoke from a fire. But then she felt raindrops on her face and realized it must be a storm cloud. Dropping the rope, she ran into the house calling to Nofria, "Mother, mother, there is a storm coming."

Nofria was cooking dinner while the children played on the floor. She immediately ran for the door saying, "I must get the chickens into the farm house."

When Nofria saw the huge funnel jumping from one object to another splaying dust all around, she knew it was more than a storm cloud. She turned quickly and ran into the house to gather up the children. "Hurry, hurry, " she shouted. "It's a tornado! We must find some shelter."

As they rushed out of the house, a neighbor, Mr. Rossario, from down the road, ran up, picked up Angelina in his arms, and led them quickly to his house. "Come to our house. We may be safer if we all stay together," he shouted.

Sophie had never experienced such fear. She squeezed between her mother and Mr. Rossario, running as fast as her young legs could carry her, praying, as the rain beat against her face. At one point, the wind was so strong; she grabbed on to a tree to keep her feet on the ground. Nofria, holding Joe in her arms, ran over and pulled her from the tree, screaming, "No! No! It can crush you."

Sophie released her hold as Nofria took her hand and dragged her on. With the terrific wind, swirling of dust and pounding of hail, Sophie thought they would never reach Mr. Rossario's house. Before long, they did. It seems God did hear Sophie's prayers. The funnel split into two parts, one went east and the other twisted around and went further west. Both Mr. Rossario's house and Nofria's house were spared.

All was calm now; Mr. Rossario opened his front door. "It's gone," he said. "It's gone." All in the house came out to see the damage this terrible monster had created. The survivors from the farmhouses slowly walked down the road to find their animals.

Cows, pigs, horses and mules, many of which were picked up and trashed against barns or dropped miles away, could be seen all over the farmland. Some animals got up and walked away leisurely. Others were dead. Sophie saw chickens stripped of their feathers and trees completely uprooted from the ground. This surely was a disaster she would never forget.

Meanwhile, Salvatore was returning from Austin, and got as far as Ben's house. While working in Germany, Ben had saved enough money to buy some land and a house in Bluff Springs, which is south of Austin near Buda. His home was not far from where Sophie and her family lived. He saw Salvatore's horse and buggy beating a path home, and shouted to him "Salvatore, STOP, STOP come, stay until it passes." Salvatore pulled the buggy up and started to tie the horses to a large post in Ben's yard, hoping they would be safe. But Ben screamed out, "No, Salvatore, put the buggy and horses in the barn." Ben ran out to help him. They could hardly see what they were doing because the dust and wind were so strong.

"I must get home, Ben. My family! I'm worried," shouted Salvatore.

"You won't make it now. Wait!" answered Ben.

Salvatore stayed. When he finally made it home, he was overjoyed to see his family safe, and immediately ran down to thank Mr. Rossario for helping them.

The next day on May 5, 1922, the "Austin-American Statesman" newspaper featured the story, telling how screaming ambulances and fire trucks raced about looking for the injured and the dead. Dual paths of destruction were caused through town and Holy Cross Hall at St. Edward's College suffered over seven hundred thousand dollars of damage.

When calm finally returned, many were injured and twelve people were dead, including an entire household of five members.

Sophie felt she had seen the wrath of an angry God that day!

Chapter 5

Picking Cotton

Three months after the terrible event of May 5th, Sophie sat on the edge of her bed early one morning, thinking, "This is not something I want to do." The summer heat alone discouraged her and she had no idea what to wear. About that time, Nofria came into her room and said, "Sophie, hurry up. Your father is waiting for you."

Sophie answered, "How should I dress?"

Nofria went to her closet and pulled out a jumper-type dress with big pockets, no sleeves. She tossed it on the bed, then said, "As cool as you can." Sophie hurriedly dressed and had a quick breakfast while Nofria wrapped a lunch in some paper for both of them. They, then, walked down the long, dusty road to the Franzoni cotton fields.

August is the hottest month of the year in Texas, and picking cotton in the blazing hot sun is unbearable. But Sophie had no choice. She was given an empty potato sack and taken into a row of cotton plants by another worker. The worker began to demonstrate the routine of picking the cotton off the plant and dropping the ball into the bag. The speed at which the worker moved took her breath away. Sophie watched her as she fought off tiny bugs. She noticed also that her fingers were bleeding from the pricking of the plants' hulls. Perspiration dripped from her brow and other places. She wanted to run away.

Sophie was also told that she would have to meet a quota for each day. Cotton-field owners depended on a certain quantity to be picked and baled. The day's amount determined how much money was earned. Each worker was paid by the pound collected. Therefore, a consistent rhythm and pace were very important to meeting the demand. As she looked around at the abundance of cotton flowing all around the land, she wilted and tears filled her eyes.

At the end of the most excruciating day of her life, she and her father walked home trying desperately not to collapse. Sophie said, "I don't want to do this kind of work, Father."

Salvatore answered, "Neither do I, Sophie. If we do not make good in one year, we will return to Michigan." Desperation did come to Salvatore and his family, but it was three years before Sophie's parents returned to Michigan.

Also, Sophie's dream of seeing Tina again dissolved. She had learned through a casual conversation with one of the workers that Tina was sent to live with an aunt in Arizona, because of an asthmatic condition. Consequently, Sophie saw Tina only once after beginning her job in the cotton fields. The families ran into one another at church. Sophie was allowed to ride home with her from church, but that evening Tina returned to Arizona.

Sophie did not know then that she would never see Tina again. As Sophie's relationship and friendship with Tina ended so did her youth. Another aspect of her life began that plunged her into adulthood much too soon.

18

Chapter 6

Ben Nardecchia

Ben Nardecchia was born to Joseph and Virginia Nardecchia, in L'Aquila, Italy, March 1892; Ben was the third child of six children. Farming was their only means of survival and he yearned for a better life. He had little or no education and never learned to read or write, but he was determined to explore possibilities that existed in another land.

Since Mussolini's association with a group of revolutionaries in the early 1900s set the political stage that Italy would eventually follow, it became clear to most young men Ben's age that military life was on the horizon. So, at age sixteen, the handsome young man with fair skin, light brown hair, undoubtedly strong both physically and mentally, decided to take his departure.

On a cold, rainy, April morning in 1908, the same year Sophie was born, Ben packed a bag and walked away from his home in L'Aquila. Being a young man, he encountered many people along the way who were friendly, willing to feed him and give him a place to sleep. It was during this time, that he met Sergio, traveling in a wagon with a caravan of wanderers.

Sergio was eighteen, very good-looking with tousled

black hair that framed his constantly smiling face. His good looks and friendly personality attracted women easily and he purposely became acquainted with all the caravan travelers. So, upon seeing Ben curled up in a corner of the wagon, he made a point to meet him. "La cigaretta?" said Sergio.

This was a welcomed sight to Ben, since it had been weeks since he smoked a cigarette. Ben said, "Grazie." Sergio inched his way next to Ben, sat down and said, "Where are you going?"

"I don't know," said Ben.

Sergio took a long, serious look at Ben and then said, "What's your name?

"Benedetto Nardecchia," he answered.

"I am Sergio Franzoni," extending his hand in friendship. "I'm on my way to Hamburg, Germany. There are large freighters there, and I understand they are in need of stevedores. "Want to come with me?"

Ben stared at Sergio a moment and then replied, "Pay is good, No?"

Sergio said, "Very good, and you only work each day until sundown."

"I go," said Ben.

As they talked, they both agreed that Hamburg would be a temporary place to live, keeping in mind their final goal of America. Traveling by wagon, or whatever means of transportation they could find, they talked to many who told them they had heard that America was truly the land of opportunity, but to go penniless was foolish. Stevedores were paid well and since Hamburg was the third largest port in the world, it was certainly a good place to start.

Caravan traveling for Ben and Sergio ended on a farm near a small French town called Berre' near Marseilles. After a lengthy discussion with the farmer, he finally agreed to exchange a horse for some farm work. The farmer's wife fixed them a meal and they slept in the barn that evening.

They arose before dawn and rode, piggyback, for miles and miles over both flat land and mountainous terrain. They discovered the farmer was not as generous as they thought for the horse was old and needed to rest quite often. Sergio and Ben would dismount and crawl under a tree and sleep.

When they finally arrived in Hamburg, they were hungrier than tired. It was mid-afternoon and they could see the large freighters docked in the harbor. Ben said, "Where do we go?"

Sergio looked around and replied, "Over there where the freighters are."

They tied the horse to a post, with the hope he would be gone when they returned, and wandered over to the docks. They were impressed with the hustle and bustle of the city.

Looking for employment, Sergio and Ben ascended the ramp of one of the large freighters docked in the harbor, called The Augustina. Sergio motioned to a sailor with a red, striped shirt and kerchief around his neck. "Il Capitano?" he asked.

"I don't know," the sailor answered. "Try the tavern on the corner."

They entered the saloon and found it noisy and crowded with sailors enjoying the freedom and merriment of land after spending weeks, maybe months out at sea. They walked up to the bar and Sergio said to the bartender, "Italiano?"

The bartender answered, "I speak some. "

"Qui cosa prende?"

Ben thought about what he wanted then laid two coins on the bar. "Due birre piacere."

The bartender returned with the two beers, and Sergio then asked in English, "Where is your Captain?"

The bartender pointed to a large man sitting at a table in the center of the room wearing a captain's hat. Ben looked over at the large man and noticing a bottle of red wine on his table, asked the bartender for a bottle of red wine.

The bartender handed Ben the wine and they walked over to the captain. Ben set the bottle on the table and said, "You speak Italian?"

The captain answered, "No. You speak English?"

Sergio replied, "Some."

The captain, showing no signs of appreciation for the wine, poured himself a glass, knowing quite well why he was being entertained. Sergio began to speak and the captain stopped him by saying, "Be at the docks tomorrow at six o'clock, and be ready to work long hours. If you need a place to sleep and eat, see Joe, the bartender. He can tell you where to go."

The next morning at exactly six o'clock, Sergio and Ben arrived at the dock of The Augustina, and began lifting and loading cargo. The first few days were grueling and difficult, driving both men practically to the point of collapse. However, their determination and perseverance enabled their strong minds and bodies to withstand the excessive labor and exertion. They worked long hours, starting at six o'clock and ending, sometimes, at eight o'clock in the evening. This would go on for six days a week, earning just a few marks a day. But, they needed the money.

Finally, after a year of this routine, about the year 1911, Sergio decided to make a move. He and Ben were sitting on a dilapidated porch on the outside of their room. They had managed to save a little money and Sergio said to Ben, "This guy at work?"

Ben said, "Yeah!"

"He says, immigrants leave all of the time from Bremer for America. They call it Bremerhaven."

Ben stared at Sergio for a moment, and then said, "Where is Bremerhaven?"

"You know the next seaport? That's it!" Sergio excitedly said. "He is going and I am going with him, Ben. Will you come with me? I have heard about this place called Texas where there's a lot of cheap farmland."

Ben said, "When?"

Sergio flipped his cigarette over the railing of the porch and turned to Ben. "Tomorrow."

They talked for a long time; Sergio explaining to Ben how he and his companion planned to hide on the ship heading for America. Excess bundles of coffee and tobacco were sent over to Bremerhaven once a week and it was his friend's assignment to deliver them safely. He simply would ask the captain for a helper or maybe two; thus, their get-away! Deliver the goods, sneak on board the immigrant ship and "Benissimo!" America! However, to Sergio's surprise and disappointment, Ben said, "No- too soon."

Ben was not as carefree as Sergio. He was positive and very serious about his plans. He did not want to go to

America penniless. He thought long and hard about buying some land to farm, finding a wife, and raising a family. He needed more money to help attain his dreams, and felt he would have to work the cargo ships a while longer.

Sergio left his good friend disappointed, but his plan was accomplished, and he arrived in America safely.

Ben continued to work and live in Hamburg, Germany, for a few more years. Sergio would write to him, encouraging him to come to America, but he never answered the letters since he was unable to write. He would have one of the sailors, who had been educated somewhat, read the letters to him.

After Sergio left, Ben heard of an empty flat from the bartender at Franz's. He and several of the cargo workers would drop in Franz's saloon every evening at the end of a long, hard day for drinks. This particular evening, the bartender leaned over to Ben and said, "You looking to move, I hear?" Ben didn't quite understand him, and so again, he said, "You gonna move?"

Then Ben got the idea, and said with a shrug of his shoulders, "Rent's too high."

"There was a man in here yesterday, a fellow about your age, Ben, looking for someone to take his flat. It is not far from here."

Ben listened and got most of what the bartender was saying, and then he asked, "This guy, will he come in tonight?"

"Maybe, Ben," the bartender answered.

So, Ben hung around for awhile sitting quietly at the bar,

since there was a language barrier and he didn't always understand what was being said. German was predominately spoken, and in the time he lived in Hamburg, he had picked up a few words. However, he was totally lost in lengthy conversation.

It was getting late and as he slipped down from the barstool, he heard the bartender yell, "Hey you, come here." At first, Ben thought he was talking to him, but then saw him motion to a guy that just came into the saloon.

"You need someone for your flat? Talk to Ben here." With that, the bartender moved on to another customer. Ben extended his hand, and to his relief, the man spoke Italian, as well as German. It turned out, the flat was on Reichter Street, just three blocks away from Franz's saloon and the rent was six marks ($5.00 a month). Ben was paying more at his present place. The gentleman took Ben over to the landlord that night and he moved in a few days later. There was something about the landlord that worried Ben. He couldn't quite put his finger on it.

While Italy rumbled with impending war, Germany thundered with it. Germany and Russia were quarreling over a number of incidental circumstances for many years; both countries flexing their muscles over who was the stronger of the two. Germany was known to have the greatest and most efficient fighting army on the earth, while their navy stood second only to the British. German settlers were scattered throughout the five continents, and the expansion of Germany became a world wonder. Russia, to the contrary, was a fifth-rate power, with first-rate desires.

Tension was all over Germany. It was one of the worst

depressions any country has experienced before or since. Although, work may have increased because of the demand for ammunition and equipment, the people and the country were in ruins. Consequently, an inner war grew in Hamburg and all of Germany. Ben was working longer hours under the worst of conditions and he began to think that not going with Sergio to America was a mistake. Also, hatred was beginning to fester because relations between Hungarians and Italians were fragile and Ben became a victim of the contempt Germans and Hungarians had toward Italians.

One evening, around nine o'clock, Ben entered the foyer of the building in which he was living. He was hungry and extremely tired. As he put his key into the lock of his door, he turned suddenly to find Mr. Grismore, the landlord, standing in the corner of the hall "Dago, want you out by Saturday!" He said cruelly.

"I pay my rent," said Ben.

"Don't want any Dagos in here, you smell up the place. I run a clean establishment."

"Why did you give me the empty flat, if you want me out now," asked Ben.

"Never mind, be out by Saturday," Grismore said scornfully.

Ben found out later that a Hungarian freight worker was there that morning looking for a flat and Grismore told him Ben was moving.

The next morning, Ben reported on the docks in a desperate frame of mind, wondering what he should do. With his mind in turmoil, he had lost his concentration while attaching a large shipment to a crane. He forgot to double-knot the rope, and as the crane swung away from him, the large crate carrying heavy guns slipped out of the rope and struck him across the head, knocking him down. He was bleeding and unconscious for some time. Two workers ran to his rescue, picked him up and laid him on a plank nearby. One of the men then ran for a bucket of water and applied cold compresses to his head. As the Captain examined Ben, he began to come around, which relieved everyone, and he was taken over to a corner of the ship to rest for awhile.

He thought he was okay and tried to get up, but he found his head spinning and his vision blurry. He became disoriented and fainted. When he awoke, he was in the Captain's quarters, lying on his bunk. "What's the problem, Ben? Never known you to have trouble tying up crates before."

Ben said nothing at first, just rubbed his head. Then he said, "I can't see too good. My eyes bother me." The captain waited a second and then said, "Think you better see the ship doctor, Ben."

The captain called one of his men and told him to take Ben to the doctor's quarters, and to report back here after the doctor was through. Twenty minutes later, Ben and the other worker returned, and told the captain that Ben was instructed by the doctor to go home and rest. He would be okay in a few days. "Need someone to get you home, Ben? Ben answered, "No."

The next morning, Ben awoke with a tremendous headache. His vision was still slightly blurred, but he felt strength in his hands and legs and decided to sit on the edge of the bed. As he was collecting himself, there was a tap at the door. He rose slowly, managed to get his pants on and answered the knock. Ben was not surprised to see Mr. Grismore. "Just thought I'd remind you that tomorrow's Saturday. You owe a month's rent, so pay up."

Ben thought for a moment, and then remembered he had paid him a week ago, when he got his wages. Ben stared him square in the eye, and said, "Don't owe you nothing. I paid last week."

Grismore's quick, sarcastic answer was "Where's your proof?" He knew Ben had no proof, because Grismore never documented his rent payments or gave receipts.

Ben had seen a couple of thugs hanging around the building more than once, and it entered his mind immediately that he could be their next victim. He slammed the door in Grismore's face, and headache or no headache, decided it was time to leave.

He threw together his belongings, and slipped down some back stairs that led to an alleyway. When he peeked around the corner of the building, he saw Grismore talking to his thugs. He decided to stay right were he was until they parted. Several minutes later, they were gone and he ran as fast as he could to Franz's saloon.

After a couple of beers, Ben settled down and began to think things through. He became aware the thugs would know where to find him. Grismore would certainly give them a lead to his whereabouts. Maybe, now was the time to go back to his ship and make plans for America.

As Ben slipped off the barstool, he turned to find Grismore's bullies standing behind him. The short, squatty one made a lunge for Ben, while the taller one came from behind, and wrapped his arm around Ben's throat. Ben reached up to release his arm from around his throat when the other punched him in the stomach. Ben doubled over in pain and a sharp crack came down on the back of his neck, which caused him to drop. The thugs ran off.

At this point, the bartender came around the bar to assist Ben, thinking he was unconscious. Ben was down but still conscious. In pain, he pulled himself up, reached for his bag of belongings, and left.

His head was pounding and his vision was bad. He could hardly see where he was going. "Where am I," said Ben out loud, trying desperately to read the street signs. People passing by saw him swaying and staggering, and assumed he was drunk. Finally, Ben could not go on any longer, and he wandered into an alleyway. He dragged his painful body to a small doorway and collapsed.

Chapter 7

Mariska and Rupert

"Can you hear me? Are you all right?" Ben could hear this voice calling down to him, but he was unable to open his eyes. He turned over and moaned. "Thank God, you are alive," said the voice. "Please, let me help you. Come into my store. I have a cot in the back room and you can rest there." Ben managed to lift his body off the ground while the other man tried to hold him steady.

"I can't open my eyes. I can't see," Ben kept repeating. Rupert directed him to the cot.

Mariska and Rupert Stegman owned a jewelry store on the corner of Market and Glashütten Streets. The store was their whole life, and they had been making a comfortable living in it for thirty years. They were sincere, kind people who loved Germany, but hated what was happening to their homeland.

In all their years there, this was the first time they had found anyone curled up against their back door in such a condition. Rupert turned to Mariska and said, "Run down the street, Mariska, and see if you can get Dr. Eiler to come. This man needs help." Mariska responded immediately and not long after, she and the doctor appeared.

Dr. Eiler examined Ben and told him he had received

some serious blows to his head, but his vital signs were normal. "He needs rest and it is important he lie very still for a couple of days." Said Dr. Eiler. "He should be able to open his eyes tomorrow, and his vision should return before long. Mariska, give him some of your good food. That should take care of him. Today, is Saturday, have him come see me in a few days."

Ben could not have had better care. The days until he saw Dr. Eiler were spent resting and eating. Mariska, her graying hair dangling on her forehead, cleaned and freshened the house constantly. Then, adjusting her glasses that always hung on the tip of her nose, would run to help Rupert in the jewelry store.

She made sure he had clean bedding and put fresh flowers in his room twice a week. He had been eating German food at cheap diners and had no idea that potato soup, sauerkraut and sauerbraten, Mariska's specialties, could taste so heavenly. Ben also noticed his headaches were beginning to disappear and his eyesight was not as blurry. The care was curing him.

One afternoon, Ben asked Rupert if he could do anything for him in the jewelry store. "I owe you my life, and would like to pay you in some way."

Rupert handed him a broom and with a big, generous smile, said, "We could use a janitor."

Ben never returned to the docks, since he had no desire to continue that part of his life. He cleaned and helped around the jewelry store, but his dream for America remained. He often talked to Rupert and Maiska about it, and after a year decided to go. Rupert helped him obtain his visa through friends and associates.

Ben first had to travel to a town called Bruckhausen, which is a suburb of Dusseldorf, Germany. Records show that Ben left Bruckhausen in February of 1911. It is not clear as to how he got there, but it is certain that Rupert arranged some means. Dusseldorf has large steamships and chemical industries, as well as a Rhine River port. Foreign trade was and still is carried on because of the city's excellent harbor facilities.

From the Rhine River port, he was transported to Rotterdam, in the Netherlands, which is quite accessible, and from there boarded an American Steamship called the SS Pennsylvania.

Without Rupert and Mariska, Ben never would have obtained his dream.

They were a wonderful part of his life. He would always remember them.

Sophie became another part.

Chapter 8

Lena Again

Nofria's six o'clock routine called for something special this morning as she sat at her sewing machine. She needed to sew the ribbons on the baby bonnet she had just completed for the layette; the new arrival would be soon. As she bent over her sewing basket, a sharp pain shot through her abdomen. She grabbed the chair and hung on tightly, waiting for the next stab. As she anticipated, it came, this time however, even stronger. In fact, it took her to her knees and she screamed for Salvatore. Nofria was very familiar with labor pains, and there was no mistaking their arrival.

Salvatore jumped out of bed and ran for the sewing room. He immediately lifted Nofria from her knees and helped her to the bedroom, got her into bed and ran three houses down the road where Mary, the midwife, lived. Mary pulled the covers down, examined Nofria and sent Salvatore for a pitcher of warm water and a basin; yelling back to him not to forget plenty of clean, white towels. Salvatore knew where everything was kept because Nofria schooled him over and over.

The labor was hard and excruciating, but thankfully, not long. A beautiful baby girl, weighing about six pounds, was born at twelve o'clock noon, exactly. As Nofria slept,

Salvatore helped Mary wash the baby in light oil. After her bath, Salvatore wrapped her in a blanket and sat in his rocking chair, holding her close. As he watched her suck her fingers, he thought how much she resembled their first little girl, Lena, who died right, after she was born. So, he said out loud, "Again, it will be Lena." And so, Lena it was! Nofria saw no reason to object.

When Lena was born in 1920. Sophie was twelve years old, and really not too concerned about the new family member. She wanted an identity and a better life than picking cotton. She missed school and she hated the idea that her family thought she did not need any more schooling after the fifth grade. Nofria reminded her she was helping the family income and that was important. Tearfully, she dragged her empty bag behind her each day to the cotton fields.

Sunday helped to improve Sophie's disposition, because it was the highlight of the week. Folks would climb into buggies, attend church, and shop at Fazio's grocery store in Del Valle, which was about six to ten miles away from Austin. It really isn't known how this tradition got started, except that perhaps it was the only grocery shopping day available for the families. The men worked the fields all week, and long hours prevented them from driving miles to a store. Very few women in those days would even consider it.

It became a weekly occurrence for all the cotton field workers and the farmers to meet at Fazio's store. Virginia Fazio was short, round and wonderful. Everyone loved her charm and she made a special effort to keep her customers happy. Extra pieces of salami were wrapped in their packages; an extra green pepper here and an extra potato there kept them coming back. Nofria was ecstatic when she found a little bag of delicious almond cookies among her groceries. "These are for me," she said to herself, and looked for a good hiding place. She made a point to tell all her neighbors and friends about Fazio's, and they too, looked for their little extra treat each time they shopped.

Sophie would see Ben periodically at the store. Sometimes, she didn't go with her parents. Sometimes, Ben wasn't there. When they did see each other, they would chat lightly. Once, Salvatore even asked Ben to bring his parents and brother, Gaetano (Guy), over for dinner. Guy was five years younger than Ben. He and his parents had arrived from Pennsylvania a few months before and decided to live with Ben. Sophie was uncomfortable with the invitation when she first found out, but it all went well.

She listened as Ben told Salvatore that he had a sister, Domenica (Mini), and a brother, Fabio, living in Pennsylvania. It seems Mini was responsible for bringing his brother, Guy, and his parents to America.

Ben told them how Mini was approached a couple of years ago after church one Sunday by promoters in the L'Aquila region. It was either 1917 or 18. Ben wasn't sure. They were sent over to entice the Italians to sail for America. Leaflets were handed out after Mass and flyers were dropped from airplanes singing the praises of the United States and the Statue of Liberty. Her interest was peaked and she decided to investigate the possibility of going to America.

After checking with the Consulate Office in Rome, she discovered it was not as difficult to make the journey as she anticipated. America was actually looking for Italian immigrants to cultivate vast areas of undeveloped land, and would give small amounts of property, ranging from thirty to sixty acres to individuals to grow fruits and vegetables.

She, then, decided to check with the travel bureau in charge and found they could make the journey, but a steerage fee was required. Not knowing where Ben was at the time, she contacted Fabio in Pennsylvania, who had found his own way to America somehow a few years before. Luckily, the United States had reduced the steerage fee to an affordable rate and Fabio sent her the money. The voyage took one month. She found her way to Pennsylvania to see Fabio and remained.

Sophie and her parents were very interested in the story Ben told, and from time to time she would catch him staring at her as he talked. She would drop her eyes and blush, but certainly liked being singled out by Ben. She noticed how good-looking he was regardless of how young she was, and her heart jumped for joy when he suggested they come to his house the following Sunday. She also noticed how much Nofria and Salvatore enjoyed his company.

Sophie's laborious walk every day to the cotton fields became beyond her endurance. She was close to fourteen years old and, other than visiting Fazio's on Sunday, there absolutely was nothing social in her life. She had no girlfriends, no one her own age to draw ideas or influences from. The younger members of her family depressed her simply because they signified more work - feeding them, bathing them, playing with them. Now, another bit of unwelcome news; Nofria was pregnant again. She could see no life of her own. Matters just got worse.

Sophie knew Ben almost two years now, and they saw each other often at Fazio's store. She knew he thought she was pretty. Her mother allowed her to be fashionable, within their means, of course; so, she had long beautiful curls and wore large hats, lots of organdy and lace dresses all which Nofria sewed. She was a joy to dress and sew for because she was so pretty. Ben had seen her mostly in her cotton field clothes, which were not very attractive, so he was amazed at her beauty when she dressed up on Sundays.

One night, after Sergio and Ben had worked a long day lifting equipment and cleaning the cotton gin, they decided to have a few beers after work. Sitting at a bar, Sergio could see Ben was distraught and he said, "Do you want to talk?"

Ben said, "Yes." He lit a cigarette and thought for awhile, then said, "Sergio, I am twenty-nine years old. It is a time for me to take a wife."

Sergio smiled and wanted to know who. "Chi?"

Ben answered, "Sophie Rizzo."

Sergio replied, "Ask her! Although, she is very young."

Ben said, "I must speak to her father first. It is the proper thing to do."

"And what do you want me to do, Ben?" asked Sergio.

"Will you come with me?" asked Ben.

Sergio said, "Sure!"

The next evening, Sergio and Ben knocked on Salvatore and Nofria's door. Sophie opened the door slowly and seeing the two men, shyly, lowered her eyes and motioned them to come in. Ben smiled at her and said, " Hello, Sophie."

She raised her eyes to him and said, "Hello."

Sergio said to Sophie, "Sophie, can we speak with your

father?"

"Come in, I will get him for you," she replied.

Salvatore was surprised to see the two young men and was unable to anticipate why they were there. Always the gentleman, he extended his hand to welcome them and said," Is something wrong?"

Sergio smiled and said, "No, no, mi scusi, Benito wants to talk to you."

Salvatore led Ben into Nofria's sewing room and, for some reason, Sophie became suspicious of something going on there. She decided to hide under the window outside on the porch, hoping Salvatore wouldn't see her. She could hear the conversation well.

Ben was saying, "Grazie. Thank you for talking to me." After a slight hesitation, he said, "I want to marry your daughter, Sophie. I am at an age where I would like a wife, and Sophie pleases me."

Salvatore was taken back with this request and, at first, was at a loss for words. He thought for a long time and then said, "Benito, do you know how old she is?"

Ben replied, "It doesn't matter."

"But, it does matter to me," said Salvatore. She is underage! Come back when she is old enough to marry."

Ben stared at Salvatore for a long while, and then said, "I am ready to marry now, if you do not let it be Sophie, then I will have to leave to search for someone else."

Salvatore replied, "Then, you will have to leave."

Sophie was livid when she heard this. Salvatore dismissed Ben without even consulting her! Here was an opportunity to change her life and free her from the cotton

38

fields! He had no right to dismiss him like he did.

If Ben left, she would lose him forever, and she really liked him. So, in her panic, she decided to write Ben a note and slip it to him when they are at Fazio's store on Sunday. She hurried back to her room quietly, so Salvatore and Ben would not see her.

As was the usual routine on Sunday morning, Sophie and her family began to dress and ready themselves for church and Fazio's store. Sophie was very nervous, but determined to carry out her plan. Inwardly, she was praying that Ben would be at the store. She must get the note to him before he leaves to find another wife.

With shaky fingers, Sophie stuffed the note into the small drawstring purse that Nofria had made for her.

Salvatore called Sophie and said everyone was ready to leave and to please hurry. Some time later, they entered Fazio's store and the usual chatter between friends began. She did not see Ben, and decided to amble slowly around the store, pretending to look over the produce.

Suddenly, she heard the bell jingle on the door as a customer came in, and somehow knowingly, suspected it was Ben. She turned; he spotted her immediately and walked over to her. Without the slightest hesitation, Sophie pulled the note from her purse and slipped it into his hand. Sophie had known Ben casually now over two years and never, at any time, had any indication that Ben could not read and write. He glanced down at the note in his hand, and slowly put it into his pocket.

When Ben returned home, he pulled the note from his pocket and thought, "Who can I get to read this for me? Sergio is not here." Sergio had left with his father the Friday before to see a man in Houston about some new equipment for the cotton fields.

As he was struggling with this thought, he saw the mailman depositing mail in the box. He didn't know him that well, but he had helped Ben decipher mail before. Would it hurt to ask him to read Sophie's note? Ben opened the door of his house and called to the postman. Coming up to the porch, Ben handed the note to the mailman and said, "Please, can you read this?"

The mailman, looked at Ben first and then at the note, and read.

Don't leave without me, Sophie

Ben's heart jumped for joy! "Grazie" he said to the mailman. "Tomorrow, when you come, will you write a note for me?" The mailman said yes, and Ben ran off, yelling "Domani - Grazie" Tomorrow - Thank you!

That evening, while lying in bed, Ben mentally prepared his note for Sophie. He had a savings from the money he earned in Germany, which helped him buy a used Model-T Ford from a friend, so, he decided to use the car for their escape. When the mailman arrived, Ben handed him a piece of paper and pencil, and said, "Please write:

My car will be parked behind your house
tomorrow night at midnight. Watch for
blinking lights. Come quickly!

The next day at the cotton fields, Sophie saw Ben hiding behind a large oak tree. As she went by, he slipped the note to her. That evening she read the note in her room. The next night, way beyond midnight, Ben sat in his car flashing his headlights, but Sophie never appeared. She was too afraid to leave her house at midnight and walk the long distance in the dark to where the car was parked.

Ben had no idea why Sophie didn't show up. He simply thought she had changed her mind. He felt rejected, but then again, maybe something prevented her from getting away. As he allowed many thoughts to roll over and over in his mind, he finally decided he would try again. If he did not receive any encouragement from her the next time, he would then move on as he had told Salvatore.

As he tried to compose a note to Sophie in his mind the following morning, he saw the postman approach. "Hello, do you need any more of my help?" the mailman asked.

"I need to write Sophie again, but don't know what to say," said Ben. Ben told him about Sophie not showing a few nights ago, and that he wanted to try one more time. "I think I will take my horse this time," Ben said. The postman sat down on the porch next to Ben, took out a pencil and wrote the following note on a slip of paper.

Will be behind the oak tree on a horse.
Watch for the wave of my hand. Drop your
bag and jump on the horse.

"Where are you taking her after you ride off?" Asked the postman.

"I don't know," answered Ben. "Bring her to my house," said the postman. "I live right up there at the top of the hill.

No one will ever suspect."

Everything fell into place as Ben had hoped. Sophie was at Fazio's store on Sunday. He slipped her the note when she wandered behind the cheese counter. After reading it quickly, she turned to him and motioned approval. Again, Ben's heart jumped for joy, and he left the store with wild anticipation.

Chapter 9

The Elopement

In Ben's mind, the plan was solid if Sophie followed the instructions of the note. She usually finished in the cotton fields by five o'clock, so he decided to be at the field by four-thirty. He was nervous, but determined. Sophie was also nervous, but determined to go through with the plan no matter when Ben arrived.

The next morning, Nofria began her usual kitchen routine of fixing breakfast. The children, Angelina, Joe and Lena were on the floor playing with a rag doll Nofria had made. Lena was close to ten months old and attempting to walk. As Nofria bent down to lift Lena into the high chair Salvatore had made for her, Sophie entered the kitchen. She was dressed in the usual clothing that she wore working in the cotton fields.

Joe was feeling feisty, throwing a piece of bread at Angelina. She screamed to gain attention, mostly, but Sophie was on edge, so she slapped Joe across the face and he began to cry. Nofria was conditioned to the children's behavior and hardly noticed their raucous morning romps, but this was the first time Sophie had reacted to them in such a manner. She was suspicious of her daughter's reaction and wondered why Sophie was so tense.

Sophie did not want her mother suspicious of anything so she decided not to wait for Salvatore, but left the house quickly and walked her usual routine down the road to the cotton fields. Her mind was confused and anxious. "Should I be doing this? She asked herself. Ben is a good looking man, but I hardly know him." She thought about so many things, but finally, decided that she could not endure the cotton fields any longer. This was an opportunity to change her life for the better, and she was going to do it!

She worked hard all day, sweating profusely and fighting ticks. Her fingers ached and she was more than convinced that she had made the right choice. There was no turning back. She would drop her bag as Ben instructed, jump on the horse and together they would ride away. The consequences of this bold act never entered her mind. She only wanted to escape.

Nervously, Ben took his watch from his vest pocket and saw that it was four o'clock. He needed a little time to saddle up a horse, and talk to the mailman one more time before arriving at his house with Sophie. He prayed silently that she would not change her mind.

He saw the postman at the mailbox, and signaled to him from the window. Ben, overly excited, said, "Today, it is today that Sophie will become my wife. We will ride from the cotton fields to your house and arrive about five thirty, maybe, six o'clock. Okay?"

The postman remembered and said, "That's fine. See you later!"

Ben arrived at the fields on horseback right on the dot at four thirty and parked behind a huge oak tree. Sophie saw him wave his hand. She left her workstation at five o'clock, directed her course right to the oak tree and dropped her bag as Ben came galloping toward her. He reached down and lifted her behind him. It was done! With the wind in her hair and the speed of the horse, Sophie had made a giant leap into adulthood.

They rode swiftly down the dusty roads. Ben was taking the course to Del Valle where the postman lived. As they climbed the hill to the postman's house, the horse began to stumble on the rocks, frightening Sophie half to death. However, Ben, being an excellent horseman, guided the horse successfully to the top.

The postman rushed out, helped Sophie down from the horse and hurried her into his house. The postman's wife, seeing how matted and soiled Sophie looked, asked if she would like to wash up; supper would be ready soon. The impact of what they had done began to surface, and Sophie cried.

Salvatore and Sophie would always meet in the office and walk home together after work. Salvatore waited around a while, but there was no sign of her. Finally, he left the office and looked for some of her co-workers. Noticing that all the workers were gone except one, looking over the production for the day, Salvatore approached him. "Sophie, go home early?" He asked.

"I don't know," he said. "I didn't see her."

Salvatore was a gentle man with a wonderful sense of humor and did not get angry quickly, but this worried him. He had wondered that morning why she left quickly without waiting for him, but he sloughed it off. Also, knowing how

Sophie felt about the cotton fields and how independent she could be at times, he began to think she might have just decided to go home without telling him. If this happened to be the case, he would indeed be angry! He stalked out of the door and rushed home with every intention of scolding her severely when he got there.

When he entered the house through the back door, Nofria was stirring spaghetti sauce on the stove. She turned, saw the anger in his face and said, "What's wrong? Where's Sophie?"

With this question, Salvatore stopped dead in his tracks and said, "You mean she's not here?"

Nofria shook her head no.

They began to panic. Sophie never delayed getting home from work and she always waited for Salvatore in the office. Nofria called to Grandma to watch the children as she and Salvatore rushed out the door to the neighbors' houses. No one had seen her.

They jumped into the buggy and Salvatore drove wildly with no idea as to where they were going. Finally, Nofria yelled in his ear, "Try Fazio's Store."

Salvatore caught what she was saying and began to think *Fazio's Store; the loving looks at one another, the quiet conversations in the corner, Ben introducing Sophie to his family, and then asking him if he could marry Sophie.* Suddenly, Salvatore knew where Sophie was. He turned to Nofria and said, "No, not Fazio's Store, Ben Nardecchia's house." Salvatore and Nofria arrived at Ben's house around six thirty in the evening.

Ben did not want his parents involved in this planned elopement, and thus, the reason for going to the mailman's house at first, suspecting Sophie's parents would come looking for her at his house. He wanted them to be able to say, "We don't know where they are."

However, Ben got careless and thought he and Sophie could quickly ride the horse back to his house, get some clothes and items they needed and then have Guy drive them to the train station. He had decided at the last minute to take Sophie to Bastrop where they would be married.

Ben's plan backfired! While he and Sophie were in the bedroom packing, Salvatore and Nofria came in the front door. Sophie heard her father's voice, angry and excited. She and Ben hid in a closet. It's a good thing Ben had explained the whole episode to his parents and Guy, because they pretended not to know anything about their whereabouts. Sophie could hear Ben's mother say they are not here, and she did not know where they were. Salvatore threatened; informing them Ben would be put in jail for kidnapping a minor.

After Salvatore's explosive anger, he and Nofria left Ben's house. Ben tried to comfort Sophie, but she cried hysterically. They left that night for Bastrop by train and located a Justice of the Peace in town.

When the Justice of the Peace asked their ages, Sophie said she was eighteen and Ben claimed to be twenty-one.

Looking them over very carefully, he said to them, "You look more like fourteen, and you are older than twenty-one." It was obvious that they did not fool the Judge and they decided to tell him about their elopement. He did not question the marriage for it was not unusual for older men to marry young girls at that time.

So, Sophie and Ben became man and wife on August 23, 1922. After the Judge married them, he asked if they would like to stay at his house for the night and they accepted.

It is hard to conceive that just a short time ago, Sophie was a child, jumping rope in her yard and clinging to her mother while they lived the dangers of a treacherous tornado. Now, she closed a door on childhood and opened another as a wife, and all at the tender age of fourteen.

When Sophie jumped on the back of Ben's horse, she accepted the future blindly. At her young age, she could not have foreseen her wedding night, having a child or children, or the struggles and poverty that would come her way. She and Ben just did what came naturally.

She never had the opportunity to discuss a wedding night with other young girls, simply because she had little contact with other young girls. In addition, it was not common practice, at that time, to approach a parent on this subject. So, it's fair to say she was surprised when Ben expected to express love in the only way he knew how. She did not refuse him, but it took time for her to realize her duties as a wife. Now, years later, the only comment that she is willing to offer is "Ben was a very sexual man."

Salvatore and Nofria found little or no sleep that night worrying about Sophie. Nofria looked at Salvatore with sad, tearful eyes and said, "What should we do, Salvatore?" Salvatore put his head in his hands, and with great exasperation, said, "Somehow, Nofria, I know Ben Nardecchia is behind this; so tomorrow, early in the morning, we are going to Fazio's Store. Mr. Fazio may be able to help us. I'll kill that son-of-a-bitch if I get my hands on him."

The next morning after breakfast, Nofria left the children again in Grandma's care, and she and Salvatore started out for Fazio's Grocery Store.

On the same early morning, an unpredicted, unplanned event occurred. Ben and Sophie returned to Ben's house the day after they were married. Ben's parents were reluctant to accept Sophie or the manner in which this marriage was consummated.

Ben, hoping to relieve the tension, between them and the parents, suggested that he and Sophie take a buggy ride to Fazio's Grocery Store to buy something for dinner. They arrived shortly before her parents.

Mr. and Mrs. Fazio were surprised to see them together. Virginia Fazio turned to Sophie and said, "Sophie, where are your parents? Is something wrong that you are here with Ben?" Sophie was nervous and too young to know how to respond to such questions. She began to cry.

Ben answered, "We were married yesterday and her parents don't know."

The Fazios were at a loss for words. The store bell jingled on the door and Mrs. Fazio turned to see Salvatore and Nofria entering. Salvatore saw Ben and lunged at him immediately, but Mr. Fazio jumped between them. Salvatore was yelling, half in English and half in Italian, "Thief! Bastard! Crook! You stole my daughter! I'll put you in prison. You'll come out when your hair is white!"

Mr. Fazio was also yelling, "Salvatore, Salvatore. Calma, calma. Calm down. We can talk about this. They're married."

Ben, frightened, at this point, did not say a word. He could hear Sophie crying behind him. Mrs. Fazio took her aside to comfort her. Finally, Salvatore calmed down and Mr. Fazio suggested they assemble in the back of the store to talk. He suggested to Sophie and Ben that they ask forgiveness from her parents for putting them through such trauma.

Sophie lifted her head and with swollen, wet eyes, said, "I am sorry, Mother and Father. Nofria always insisted that Sophie call them "Mother and Father," and so, she did not fail them at this time either.

Ben said nothing. Salvatore could only stare at Ben in anger.

At first, Nofria hesitated to accept Sophie's apology, but she realized that the deed was done, and only requested that Sophie and Ben remarry in the Catholic Church.

Ben and Sophie honored her request by having their marriage blessed at St. Mary's Church the following December. However, Sophie will tell you that Salvatore never forgave Ben, and refused to talk to him for many years.

Ben's parents
Joseph and Virginia Nardecchia

Sophie on the right at twelve-years old with sister, Angelina
(wearing flower wreath) on her First Holy Communion.

Sophie and Ben with Aunt Minnie and Uncle August in 1922

Sophie and Ben's children in 1932
From left to right: Rose, Mary, Buddy, and Sam

Ben Nardecchia (center) pictured with other
employecs at Surebest Bakery in 1934.

Victor Nardecchia owner of the three restaurants
called *Victor's* in Austin, Texas

Sophie and her sisters:
Augustina, Angelina, Mary and her brother Joe

Sophie's brother Joe, killed in WWII at Normandy

Sophie's parents, Salvatorre and Nofria, 1946

Sophie and Ben's daughter, Lena, crowned Queen in 1951
by St. Edwards's University students.

Sophie, Ben and David in 1953

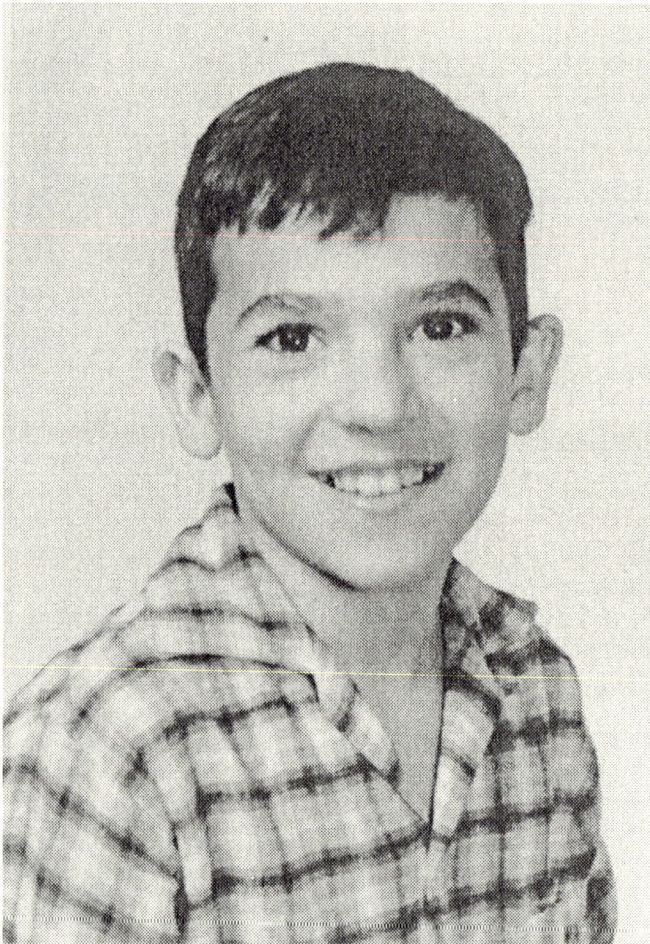

David, Sophie and Ben's youngest son, at five-years old.

Sophie in front of her home on Lake Austin Boulevard
admiring the bluebonnets.

of

VICTOR NARDECCHIA

WHEREAS, our Heavenly Father in His wisdom called unto Him our friend, Victor Nardecchia, on June 29, 1964; and

WHEREAS, Victor, as he was affectionately known among his countless friends throughout the industry, will long be remembered for his generosity, unselfishness and sincerity which endeared him to his fellow restaurateurs, as well as friends, who feel a deep personal loss in his untimely passing; and

WHEREAS, Victor was elected President of the Austin Chapter of the Texas Restaurant Association in June, 1963, and unselfishly he helped develop the largest membership ever known in the Austin Chapter; and

WHEREAS, his energy, coupled with a cheerful and sincere desire to do something for his fellowman, was perhaps his greatest attribute, and through the goodness of his heart and in trying to do something to upgrade the industry that had been so kind to him, he gave and gave and gave until the last; and

WHEREAS, Victor was held in the highest esteem by the Texas Restaurant Association, its Officers, Directors, members, staff, and by all who were privileged to know him:

NOW, THEREFORE, BE IT RESOLVED that the Texas Restaurant Association, its Officers, Directors, members, and staff, elect to let this resolution serve as their expression of unending gratitude for Victor Nardecchia's long and devoted years of dedicated service; and let this document serve as their most sincere expression of deepest and heartfelt sympathy to members of his family.

Harry A. Porter
President

(signature)
Executive Vice-President

Tribute to Victor Nardecchia presented by the
Texas Restaurant Association in 1964

Bill Church, Sophie's second husband in 1985.

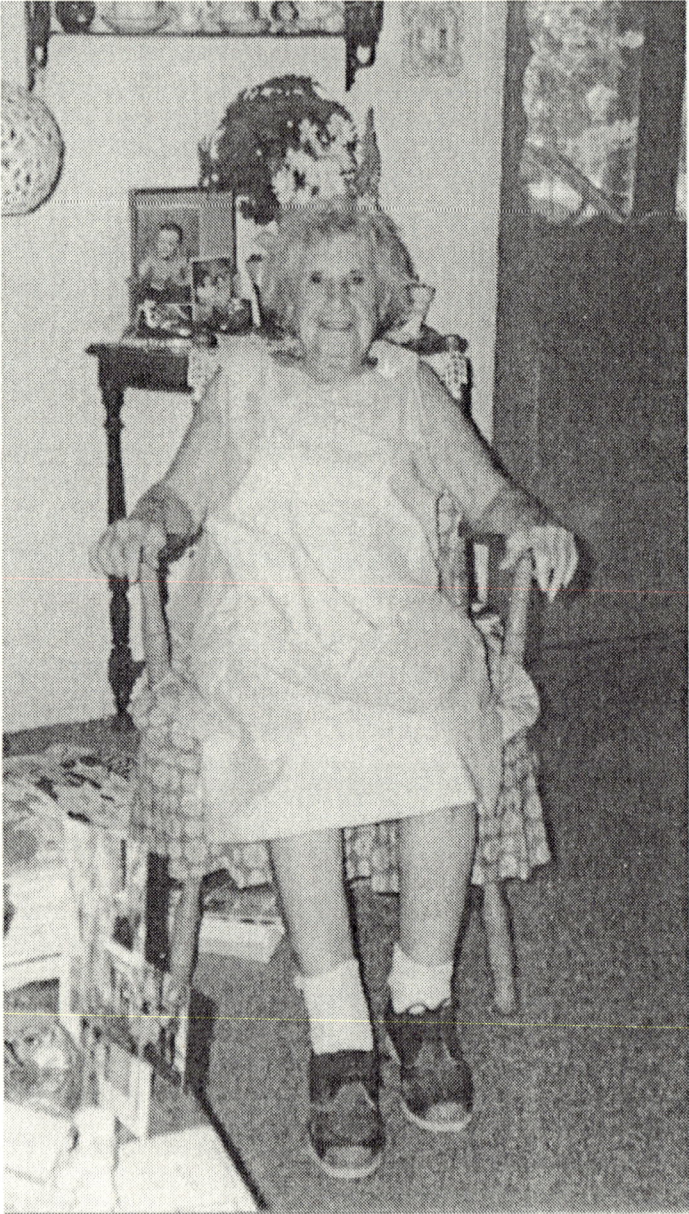

Sophie at 92 in her present home

Chapter 10

Virginia and Joseph

After their marriage, Sophie moved into Ben's house with his parents and brother, Guy. At first, happiness prevailed. Ben bought her a trunk in which to keep her personal items, because closet space was very limited, and a phonograph, because she loved music. Every evening after dinner, they would play the phonograph and dance.

She felt completely refreshed and reborn and saved from the exhausting grind of the cotton fields. She had indeed made a wise choice in eloping with Ben, and hoped some day Salvatore and Nofria would truly forgive her, but her carefree, happy-go-lucky world did not last long.

Ben had taken on more responsibility and needed to make some decisions. First, he decided to leave Franzoni's cotton fields and work his own farmland, which he did, but not with any success. The farm never prospered, growing only enough produce for them to survive but not enough to sell. Drought destroyed their crops, leaving nothing to take to market. There was no money coming in. Sophie made some small change selling fresh eggs, but not enough on which to run a household.

To make matters worse, Sophie's relationship with Ben's parents never improved. They simply distrusted her. Virginia, Ben's mother, barely spoke to her, and Joseph, Ben's father, spied on her. On several occasions, she had caught him tiptoeing down the hall to check on her when she would be sitting alone. She let a salesman into the house one day to look over his bracelets and trinkets, and as she was trying to decide what to buy, she caught Ben's father out of the corner of her eye spying on her behind a curtain.

Ben was aware of their attitude toward Sophie, and kept a close eye on the situation. At one time, they chastised her because she got her hair cut short, calling her a "loose woman." When Ben found her crying on the porch, he scolded his parents and told them to leave her alone. He liked her hair short. Ben knew this living arrangement could not last, and he would have to find an alternate.

Guy, at this point was not a problem. He had met and fallen in love with a young girl, named Jeanne. With this preoccupation, he paid board to Ben and gave little or no attention to what transpired in the household.

Meanwhile, while Ben was worrying about how he was going to support his family, he stopped in at Fazio's Store one afternoon, and met a Mr. Falwell who was looking for someone to work his cotton fields in Del Valle. He told Ben he would give him a place to live and supply him and his family with vegetables, some live chickens, and a cow, if they would work his fields.

Ben did not hesitate to accept the offer. His farm was failing miserably and he had just learned that Sophie was pregnant. Needless to say, Sophie was not happy when she learned the cotton fields had returned to her life.

The next morning, she and Ben drove to Del Valle to see the house and Sophie was devastated. There was no water, no electricity, no icebox, one large bedroom and a kitchen. How could five people and a new baby live under these conditions? But, Ben had made a commitment to Mr. Falwell and he would not go back on his word. In fact, he thought with time, he could learn the cotton business and have fields of his own.

So, obedient to Ben, Sophie and Ben's parents moved into Mr. Falwell's house. Each day again, Sophie worked the cotton fields; in addition to the daily household chores that had to be done. Ben's mother only helped with the cooking, leaving mountains of dishes to be cleaned up after supper. Water had to be carried from the well to do dishes and laundry, and sometimes she worked late into the night by a kerosene lamp, folding clothes.

Ben helped her whenever he could, but he too worked hard late at night, helping to reach the quota needed for cotton production. Ben might not have been able to read or write, but he had an inborn ability for knowing how much cotton had to be picked in order to reach production for the day. Sophie was five months pregnant and exhausted.

Chapter 11

Family Survival

Family ties were indeed broken after Ben and Sophie's elopement. Salvatore decided Texas cotton fields had done enough damage to him financially. His health had improved considerably in Texas, and since he was convinced that the dyes and chemicals in the factory were the cause of his coughing, he packed up his family and moved back to Michigan, thinking he would find a different type of employment.

Sophie was saddened by their leaving, but Salvatore was firm in his decision. Nofria had forgiven Sophie by now and they both named their new babies Mary. Salvatore never forgave Ben and left without even saying good-bye.

Ben and Sophie's financial situation was no better, maybe even worse. They lived from day to day. Their diet consisted of chicken, eggs, milk and whatever vegetables her gardens produced, and picking cotton contributed very little to the household budget. There simply was no surplus for clothing or other important necessities. Meat was a luxury, and not affordable for them.

On the occasions when they would go to Fazio's Store, only bare necessities were bought. Mrs. Fazio would give Sophie neck bones to make spaghetti sauce, or Ben would buy a bag of cornmeal to make polenta.

As their children grew, polenta became a "specialty" and they loved it. He would stir the cornmeal for hours with a long stick on top the stove until it became thick. Then, it was poured on a large board and he would cover it with sauce. Everyone was handed a spoon and they ate right off the board. A "poor man's meal" with a wealth of family togetherness!

Mary was thirteen months old when Ben and Sophie's second child was born. Sophie's delivery was much easier this time compared to the long, hard labor she endured with Mary. Her contractions started early that morning, and by the time Ben scurried to town and returned with the midwife, a healthy boy had been born.

Sophie and Ben's first son was born March 30, 1925, and his father insisted on naming him Sabatino, not only because he was born on the Sabbath Day, but Ben wanted him named after his great grandfather, Sabatino Nardecchia. Sophie was not completely sold on the name of Sabatino, so they compromised, and called him Sabatino "Buddy," and it was written exactly that way on his birth certificate. Everyone called him Buddy, except the nuns in school because they felt Buddy was not a Christian name, so they called him "Sabi."

It was at this time that Ben began to think about producing his own cotton fields. However, his dream never became a reality. Mr. Falwell offered to teach him the market, but he was too limited. Not only was he unable to read or write but his financial situation prevented him from buying the necessary equipment needed to produce cotton, the most important being a cotton gin. After the cotton is picked, it is then put in through a gin to remove all the seeds before it is baled. Then, he would also need cotton pickers, and even though they worked for little or nothing, he would still have to pass on their share of the amount per pound picked.

Ben was a poor risk for any bank simply because he had no collateral and no education. So, he continued working for Mr. Falwell, hoping against hope, something would come along to improve their conditions. From time to time, he would talk to Sophie about raising corn and selling it but she would lose interest since she could see nothing would come of it.

Ben's parents and Guy continued to live with Ben and Sophie, and the tense situation never changed. Nor did her life get any easier, especially when Mini, Ben's sister, decided to leave Pennsylvania and come to Texas, in about 1926 or 1927. She not only visited but also stayed with them for a while. Mini was a repeat of her mother and made Sophie's life miserable. She was treated as a child and both women scolded and criticized her constantly.

Mini thought she cleaned too much and Virginia spoiled the children. Mini constantly repeated the same phrase, "A dirty house makes good crops," until Sophie couldn't bear it any longer. Sophie objected to giving Mary coffee in the morning and Virginia ignored her request and poured Mary coffee every morning. She was on the point of a breakdown and discovered she was pregnant again.

Finally, after a continuous battle between the women and a miserable household, Ben talked to Mr. Falwell and he suggested that the families split up. Falwell was willing to build another house and he did. This, at least, brought relief to the situation.

However, romance made the final decision. Mini was introduced to Augostino (Augie), a cousin in the family, and after dates and attraction to each other, they married. The family objected because they were first cousins, but this fact did not matter to Mini and Augie. He and Mini were both from Pennsylvania, and they decided to leave the heat of Texas and return.

Guy, seeing that his romance with Jeanne was not progressing, made a decision to also go back to Pennsylvania as well. Sophie had learned from gossip at Fazio's Store that he proposed and that Jeanne said, "no." The disappointment affected him terribly.

Joseph and Virginia decided they did not want the tense living conditions with Sophie any longer, so they returned to Pennsylvania with Guy. However, no one could possibly know how grateful Sophie was for all the decisions that were made.

Guy and Joseph, however, did not stay long in Pennsylvania. Joseph and Virginia were having marital problems. Joseph, in his late eighties and Virginia, not much younger, began to fantasize and accuse her of having affairs with other men. Virginia, having heard this accusation over and over again, decided she could not take it any longer and moved in with Mini and Augie. Guy brought his father back to Austin and, again, they moved in with Sophie and Ben.

One evening, Guy stopped in a neighborhood saloon and struck up a conversation with two fellows sitting at the bar. He discovered they were mechanics that worked for an auto shop on Lamar Blvd. Guy mentioned he was looking for a job and they gave him the address of the shop. The next morning he applied and the boss hired him

With some of the turmoil gone from the household, Ben woke very early one morning, bathed and dressed in a shirt and tie. Sophie, who was always an early riser, watched him comb his hair as she drank a cup of coffee at the kitchen table. Finally, she said, "Where are you going?"

"Something has to change. It is not good here," Ben answered. "The corn looks very bad and there is no rain, and I am not making enough money with Falwell. Falwell said I should go to Surebest Bakery. They will pay someone to sweep and clean up the place - you know, do some odd jobs around. I go see about it."

Sophie nodded her head up and down and simply said "Good luck, Ben!" That evening, the news was good. Mr. Pauls hired Ben.

Ben and Sophie saw no problem with continuing to live where they were, even though Ben would be working part-time in Austin. Between Ben's old Ford and Guy's truck, they could drive back and forth to the city. This pleased Sophie because she didn't want to give up her gardens. She had worked so hard on them and they were producing enough vegetables to feed the family. Joseph had settled down since being separated from Virginia, and he became a big help turning the soil and planting vegetables.

Mr. Falwell also let them milk his cow for fresh milk.

They had adjusted to their environment, in spite of meager living conditions. Like Sophie told Ben, "Where else could we live and not pay rent?"

Ben, however, saw that they could not make ends meet

on the amount of money Falwell was paying him. So, being an honest man, Ben told Falwell he would be working part-time at the bakery, but he felt he could continue to work the cotton fields also. He just could not support his family on the earnings alone from the cotton fields. Mr. Falwell did not offer Ben more money and, in fact, came one day to ask them to move.

"Ben," he said. "We need to talk. It seems you're spending more time at the bakery and less time in the cotton fields. This is not the arrangement we had from the beginning. The truth is Ben, I have someone else in mind for this house, and you'll have to find other living quarters. I'm sorry!"

Sophie's eyes filled with tears as she listened to Mr. Falwell. She had delivered her third baby; a sweet little girl she named Rose. Now, again, this entire family had to pack up and move, leaving her favorite treasures behind. But, sometimes when a door closes, a window opens.

Chapter 12

Seventh Street

Ben heard at the bakery one afternoon that a large house was vacant on Seventh Street in Austin, and he mentioned this to Sophie at the dinner table one evening. The next day, they took a ride to Seventh Street to see the house, and not only were they not disappointed in its size, they were impressed with its appearance. It was an attractive white frame with a wrap around front porch. It seemed to be in good condition and they felt it would be adequate for their family.

As they peeked into the blank windows, deprived of shades and curtains, their interest was peaked and they decided to explore further. However, it was locked, and attached to the mailbox was a note saying, "Go to grocery store on corner of Sixth and Comal for key to house." The owner of the grocery store and his wife were warm, friendly people and gave Ben the key. The man who owned the house on Seventh Street lived in Waco, but business transactions for the house were done by the grocery store.

Ben unlocked the door and found that the front entrance led into a large living room. From the living room, they strolled down a long hall that led to the kitchen. The kitchen had a wood burning stove for cooking, which they later found out, also warmed the kitchen quite nicely. The hall then led to two bedrooms on the right and one on the left. The bedroom closest to the kitchen had a pot belly stove for heating. The hall then extended back to a screened-in porch and to the left of the porch was a bathroom.

Not only was the house satisfactory for a big family, it also provided Sophie with a huge backyard and the vision of a productive vegetable garden. Now all of this sounds ideal, but there were drawbacks. There was no gas and no electricity, which meant that water had to be heated on the stove for everything. When bathing the children or washing clothes, Sophie would heat hot water on the pot belly stove and carry it to the bathtub; not once but many times. Also, the bathroom off the screened-in porch in the wintertime was unheated and very cold.

Since there was no electricity, Sophie and her family lived by kerosene lanterns or went to bed before dark. Old habits are hard to die. Sophie to this day rises at five in the morning and retires by seven o'clock at night.

At first, Sophie found the deprived conditions difficult, but after a time she and Ben accepted the sacrifices because the house was affordable. The rent, was an unbelievable $14 a month. After Sophie and Ben moved into the house, payment was made each month to the grocery store. The owner, in turn, sent the amount to the man in Waco.

A long square table with benches on the side was made, either by Ben or a friend, and placed on the screened porch where the family ate their meals every day. In addition, Sophie sewed curtains for the windows and clothes for the children.

She became acquainted with her neighbors, who were

mostly African American, and kept herself busy maintaining her vegetable gardens and selling eggs that came readily from the several chickens she allowed to roam her backyard.

But every time Sophie became complacent and comfortable, another challenge surfaced. This one started out warm and easy with happy thoughts, but sadly, did not end that way. Ben and Sophie had some good friends in Del Valle and were invited to a picnic in the country. Their children were excited. Sophie, too, was ready for some pleasure in her life and visiting with friends was an ideal remedy. She and Ben packed up the kids and drove to the country.

It was a lovely summer day, yellow, red and blue flowers in bloom all along the side of the roads, and as they got closer to the country, the brilliant spray of wildflowers was breathtaking.

The children had a full day of running, playing with other children and stuffing their little faces with good food. After dinner, watermelon was served and Sophie, known to outlast anyone in the amount of watermelon that could be consumed by one person, ate more than her share. On their way home, she began to feel uncomfortable with cramps and pain. Thinking that she had eaten too much watermelon, she went to bed early with a hope she would feel much better in the morning.

The following morning was no different and her pain worsened. Ben located a neighbor to watch the children and took Sophie to the hospital. After a thorough examination, Sophie was diagnosed as having an acute appendicitis and an emergency operation was performed. The surgery was difficult and the pain severe. Sophie's complete recovery took approximately a year, and many days were very difficult trying to keep up a home and take care of the children.

She finally recovered and by 1935, the family was fully settled in on Seventh Street. Ben was steadily working at the bakery. The pay wasn't always sufficient for his family as they started to grow, but he brought home bread and sweets to help feed them. Guy helped by paying board. They had improved their financial situation somewhat, but by no means were able to feed large groups of people for long periods of time.

However, it was a custom for Italian family relatives living outside of Texas to "drop in." on one another. Each, during desperate times, helped the other to feed their families.

One day an aunt and her six children from Pennsylvania, on Ben's side of the family, knocked on their door. Sophie was surprised. Ben welcomed them with open arms. "Ciao. Come stay. How are you? Stay! Stay!"

Even though they were expected to arrive in Austin at some time, it was not known when they would arrive because of the long distance they had to travel.

They stayed for weeks. Preparing meals and entertaining, not only for their family, but friends and relatives of this family. After a while, this became somewhat unsettling for Sophie. She complained openly, and became quite unpopular with members of Ben's family. No one even realized that Sophie's behavior could have been the result of her body still in the process of healing from surgery.

The family finally did settle in Austin, staying with different relatives until they were able to make their own living. As a matter of fact, a famous family restaurant, called

Victor's Italian Restaurant, located on 23rd Street, very near the University Drag, was successfully established in 1940. Later, two other restaurants were opened bearing the same name.

Victor Nardecchia was so highly regarded by his peers that, upon his death, the Officers and Directors of the Texas Restaurant Association passed a tribute in a session of its September Board of Directors' Meeting at the Shamrock Hilton Hotel in Houston, Texas.

Sophie experienced many unsettling events in her married life that she would never had anticipated. One that stands out in her mind came a warm afternoon while she was crocheting on the front porch. It was a letter from Nofria. Sophie noticed it was from New Jersey, and this surprised her.

The letter announced that they were unable to stay any longer in Michigan because Salvatore could not find a job. They discovered a good deal of their family had moved to New Jersey, and they decided to contact a cousin, who was a manager in a toy factory to see if Salvatore could get a job there. The cousin accepted him and Salvatore again packed up his family and moved to New Jersey.

Salvatore's health had improved considerably while living in Texas, and according to Sophie, he probably felt he was cured. So, again, he returned to the toy factory. This may have been a mistake for him, but it was much later in his life that his symptoms returned.

At the time the letter arrived, Salvatore and Nofria had six children, the last one being John. Though a beautiful little boy, Sophie knew from pictures Nofria sent and the letters she wrote, he was not a healthy child. He had died young of diabetes.

Now Nofria's letter brought another tragedy. Sophie's sister, Lena, who was now thirteen years old, had died. Someone poured lye into a regular drinking glass and placed it back on the sink without washing it. Lena, thinking it was a clean glass, filled it with water and drank. The lye burned the entire lining of her throat and she died hours later.

As Sophie began to tremble and scream, a neighbor ran over and found her curled up in a corner. She grieved for months over her sister's death. She was unable to attend the funeral and this made her grief even sadder.

Both Sophie and Nofria continued to have children. All tolled, Nofria had nine and Sophie had six, not counting a little girl she lost after birth. After Rose, she had a healthy big boy they called Sammy, and then named her next baby girl, Lena, after her sister. By the time Sophie was nineteen years old, she had delivered five children. And, Sophie and Ben not only had concerns and worries over their own children, but also had additional problems with Guy and Joseph. Joseph would help Sophie with her vegetable gardens, but he was getting very senile and Guy was getting peculiar.

Sophie suspected that he never did quite get over his disappointment in love. He seemed to have a desperate look about him most of the time. When he was home, she would try to talk to him, feel him out about the things that were troubling him, but he was not responsive. He would sit in a chair and just stare. If the children became noisy, he would scream at them, become angry and slam his bedroom door. Sophie became frightened of him for herself and the children.

Then, one evening he came in after dinner and Sophie smelled a strong aroma of alcohol on him. He was swaying and she could tell he was drunk. She decided to talk to Ben about him. However, Ben was easy and simply said, "You worry too much. Guy is okay!"

There were several episodes with Guy, but Sophie is fully aware of one. They were at the dinner table one night and someone knocked on the door. Ben answered it and an older man said, "Are you Guy Nardecchia's brother, Benito?"

Ben answered, "Yes."

"We found your name and address in his pocket. He's lying on the side of the road, either dead drunk or very sick. Want me to drive you over there?" Ben grabbed his jacket and followed the man to his car. They found Guy drunk and brought him home.

Sophie and Ben began to hear tales about Guy missing work. He would tell Ben he was working, when actually, he was hanging out in a saloon with a rough crowd, smoking marijuana and drinking alcohol. Guy was old enough to determine his own life, but his behavior was affecting his family and others.

It seems he was also stalking his old girlfriend, Jeannie. He would get high on drugs and wait for her to come home or follow her during the day. One night he stood under her bedroom window yelling and calling her name. A couple of times, he approached her but she sloughed him off and he had a hard time accepting that. His obsession for her was totally out of control.

Finally, his boss at the auto shop fired him. Jeanne's father was concerned about his daughter and called Ben. He felt Guy's problems were serious, and suggested that Sophie and Ben take him to a psychiatrist. Jeanne's father even suggested he would set up an appointment for them at the State Institution for the Mentally Impaired.

Ben, Sophie and Guy went to the State Institution two days later. Guy was livid about the appointment, and chastised them for setting up an appointment. In fact, Sophie had to threaten him before he would consent to go.

"If you do not go with us, Guy, then you leave. You can cook your own meals and do your own laundry. I don't like the way you are acting around me or my children." Guy agreed to go.

After a battery of tests, the doctor suggested that he remain a few days for more testing. Sophie knew from early on that Ben could not read or write, so it was up to her to do all the necessary signing. She filled out all the forms and signed them. It is guessed that Guy did read and write, but Sophie did not know how well.

After all the tests, Guy was diagnosed as being schizophrenic, and he remained in the Institution. The doctors felt he would be a danger to others.

Sophie had difficulty sleeping many nights after Guy's commitment. She and Ben were amazed that his case was finalized so quickly. Medications were not as prevalent then for mental disorders as they are now, but Sophie always felt something could have been done that was less drastic.

Buddy was a little boy around six-years-old, at that time, and followed his dad everywhere. He even worked at the bakery with Ben at an early age. So, it was not unusual for him to accompany Ben to the Institution to visit Guy. He remembers visiting his Uncle Guy and even now will say, "He really didn't seem that bad."

After a time, Guy was moved from the Institution near 45th Street to The Old Confederate Home on West Seventh Street, which was another group of buildings, owned by the State, and was not far from where the family lived. They would all visit him often, but he died in the Home. Actually, he lived a long life there. He died after Ben, on June 9th, 1971.

When Guy passed away, a disability pension check for $1,400.00 was issued because he was a ward of the State. Sophie could use whatever she needed to bury him, but the remainder of the money had to be distributed to all of his relatives wherever they were. It became so complicated that finally, Sophie made arrangements for him to be buried at Mount Calvary Cemetery, and told the State they could have the rest. After the funeral and burial, it didn't amount to much anyway.

The family members, realizing Joseph was disoriented and getting more senile, decided to withhold the whole story from him. He wasn't aware that Guy was gone. Sophie, was pregnant during the whole trauma with her sixth child. However, she became so stressed over the whole situation that she went into early labor. The baby, a little girl, did not survive. She lived only a few hours, and Sophie named her Veronica. Her heart grieved over the loss of this child for a long time.

Since money was always tight in the Nardecchia household, Sophie decided to go to work. She had recovered from the loss of Veronica, and heard that The Austin Laundry on Lavaca Street, near the University of Texas, was hiring. They were desperately in need of an extra worker and she passed the interview with flying colors. However, as she anticipated, Ben did not approve.

"Stay home," he shouted. "Take care of our children. I work and bring home bread, cakes and lots of food for us to eat. You don't have to work!"

"We are having trouble meeting our bills," Sophie shouted back. "You don't worry when a bill isn't paid. I do! Let me try, okay? The older kids will be in school, and our neighbor, Lila, across the street said she would take care of Lena. I asked the laundry for the early shift and I should be home by two o'clock, before school is out. If it doesn't work out, I will quit." Ben said no more, but Sophie knew she had to make it work.

The first day of Sophie's job, the bluebonnets were beginning to pop out, Indian paintbrushes were swishing with the breeze, and spring was in the air. The warm breeze coming in her window woke her. Remembering her challenge for the day, she jumped out of bed and then woke Mary. Mary was eleven years old, and it was her responsibility to get Rose and Sammy off to school, while Sophie took Lena over to Lila.

Sophie found working at the laundry difficult, but she was determined to continue because of the additional money. Bills were being paid and there was less stress stretching a dollar. She was frugal, and very good at budgeting, enough so, that she saved the train fare necessary to take Lena and Sammy with her to New Jersey to visit her family.

It had been eleven or twelve years since she had seen

Nofria and Salvatore, and the long train ride was well worth the tensions encountered when traveling with children. Visiting with her family and having, at least, two of her children meet their grandparents, gave her a tremendous lift. She encouraged them to visit her soon.

After Sophie and the children returned from New Jersey, she and Ben returned to their normal routine, but Sophie began to realize that working in the laundry was grueling, and almost as bad as the cotton fields. Putting her hands in boiling hot water every day began to irritate her skin so badly that she had to see a doctor.

In addition, after arriving home from work one afternoon, Lila came over. "Sophie, Sophie, you here?" She tapped on the door and as was their custom with each other, walked in.

Sophie had just changed from her white uniform, a requirement at the laundry, and came out of the bedroom. "Hello, Lila! Thanks so much for bringing Lena home. I was just coming over to get her. Hope she was a good girl for you, today," Sophie commented.

"She's no trouble, honey, but I'm afraid I can't take care of your baby no more. You see, my George has taken a job far away, and we goin' be movin'," said Lila.

Sophie's heart sank. Lila was the only one in the neighborhood to whom she could trust Lena. She would have to leave the laundry and that decision would be reinforced when Ben was told about Lila moving.

"You quit the job, Sophie," was Ben's first reaction, and she, realizing that the job was taking a toll on her body, agreed and resigned.

Some time after she retired from the laundry, Mini and

Augie again returned to Austin. They moved into a home in the general area of West Lynn and Tenth Street. It is not really known why they decided to leave Pennsylvania and come back to Austin, but after they settled in, Joseph decided to live with them. He was quite old now and probably needed a more peaceful household with fewer children's activities. They made one more move in the same general vicinity and remained there. Joseph passed away in 1937.

Families would come and go, children got older, and Sophie and Ben swung back and forth on budgeting their income. Now that Sophie was not working, her discontentment returned. She, again, realized that there simply was not enough money to cover all the necessities. She was bothered by the fact that the children did not have shoes for school, and that Buddy had to wear his hand-me-down Boy Scout uniform every day because his wardrobe was so lean. When she and Ben shopped on payday, it had to be for one item for one child. The others simply did without until another time.

Today, as she sips her morning coffee, she thinks about these things, as well as events of the past. She knows she has a great will, but some events in her life depress her. She recalls the time she decided to carry Rose and walk several blocks to a small notions store on Sixth Street. She was very limited in her shopping since she had only small change in her purse. However, she purchased some thread, a small amount of ribbon and some elastic. She sat Rose on the counter as she paid for her items and chatted with the friendly woman at the cash register. Halfway home, Sophie began to realize how heavy Rose was getting; oh, what she would give to have a buggy! In shifting the baby from one arm to another, she discovered her purse was missing. In her panic, she rushed back to the store, but to no avail. The purse was gone.

"Do you think someone will return it?" Sophie asked the woman at the cash register.

"Maybe, but I wouldn't count on it," the lady answered.

As she carried Rose home, she remembered sobbing over the loss of a few pennies, because they had so little.

As Sophie welcomed daybreak and the peaceful quiet of the mornings, she was aware that she simply had to return to work. There was no way they could live on Ben's income. She did return to the working world, but years later when the children were much older.

Chapter 13

Brett Lane

It was a hot September. Ben made polenta in spite of the hot weather, mainly because the kids were asking for it. After Sophie finished cleaning up the kitchen, she joined Ben on the front porch. He was sitting in an old rocker and she dropped on the top stair of the porch.

She commented on the weather, "I wonder if it will ever cool off. This is September! I simply cannot take this humidity!"

Ben grunted a little. "Maybe better tomorrow."

Sophie began to tell Ben about her conference with Sammy's teacher. Sammy was not doing well in school and the teacher sent several notes home requesting a conference. Sammy was unable to offer any insight as to why the teacher wanted to see her, and so, Sophie, finally decided to attend the conference.

"They are recommending that Sammy have a special tutor to help him with his reading," Sophie told Ben. "A special tutor is very expensive and we don't have the money to do this," said Sophie.

Ben suggested that the older children help him. However, this was not the answer. He needed help on a professional level, and the older children simply became frustrated with him and quit trying. So, without personal tutoring, Sammy was just pushed along from grade to grade until he quit after completing the seventh grade. Like his father, Sammy never learned to read and his writing was very limited.

After discussing Sammy, Ben brought up a subject concerning an empty house. Mr. Hill was a driver for Surebest Bakery, and Ben had numerous conversations with him during the day. Mr. Hill also got to know Buddy who would go with Ben on Friday nights, around ten o'clock, to do miscellaneous jobs around the bakery. Then, around four o'clock in the morning, when all the bakery goods had been packaged, Bud would help load Mr. Hill's truck and travel every Saturday with him making deliveries to small towns. Bud was no more than eleven years old.

Mr. Hill also had Bud work the gardens at his home. Buddy learned at a very young age how to work and earn money.

Through this close relationship, Mr. Hill told Ben about a house he owned on Brett Lane, and Ben drove over to see the house. As he sat with Sophie on the porch he decided to tell her about the "cabin," as he called it. He was never happy with what he referred to as "pesky neighbors."

Every afternoon, from three-thirty until dinner time, two Mexican men down the block would wander down to Sophie's porch and visit with her. Then, members of the black family across the street would stroll over, and as innocent as it may have been and as innocent as Sophie may have been, Ben objected to the daily routine.
"Tomorrow, we go see the 'cabin," Ben said.

What Ben called a "cabin," was really a bungalow

located on land owned by the University of Texas. It had a living room, dining room, one bedroom, a large screened porch, and one bath. After looking the cabin over, if Sophie and Ben decided to move in, they would be required to pay the University five dollars a month for use of the land. A friendly financial agreement was made between Ben and Mr. Hill.

When Buddy heard they would probably leave Seventh Street, he objected. It meant he would not see much of his friend, Prince. Prince was a black boy living on the block, and Buddy's best friend. He and Prince would get in free every Saturday afternoon at a movie theatre on Twelfth Street, that was owned by one of the black families on their block. The highlight of their week was to watch Shirley Temple or Frankenstein. However, his objection was totally ignored by Ben and the following morning, they all went to inspect the bungalow on Brett Lane.

At first, their living conditions were cheap and mostly favorable. They had a large backyard where chickens roamed and laid eggs. Sophie started up her vegetable gardens again, and it was amazing how easily she adapted to new surroundings.

After a few months of living on Brett Lane, Sophie discovered that her neighbors, Mr. and Mrs. Bird, living behind them, had a cow. It was becoming increasingly difficult for them to get fresh milk from the farm each week, so she persuaded Ben to consider getting a cow for them. In talking with her neighbor, she discovered that Clyde Barrow of "Bonnie and Clyde," was Mrs. Bird's brother. Sophie will tell you that Mrs. Bird wore black all the time and kept a very low profile because of the shame her brother brought to the family

Mr. Bird recommended that they inquire at the farm where Ben and Sophie got their fresh milk, and after a few trips back and forth to the country, Sophie asked how they could obtain a cow. She felt it was feasible for them to have a cow because they lived in an area where there was space between their bungalow and the Colorado River, and the cow would have plenty of grass for grazing. Also, she felt satisfied that the children would have fresh milk every day.

Through their inquiry, they were able to get a reasonably priced cow, albeit the cow was old, but unbeknownst to the seller, they discovered the cow was expecting a calf. So, to keep the cow healthy, occasionally they would drive out to the country and cut Johnson grass for additional feed. Sophie sold the calf after it was born and made a neat little sum in the exchange.

After a period of time, they began to have problems with the cow. She would constantly wonder off and they would have to search for her. Then, she fell into a hole and broke her leg. She became more of a hindrance than help so Ben got rid of her. Oddly enough, Sophie never would go near the cow. She was frightened of it, so Buddy would take care of it and milk it every day.

Thinking their new living arrangements would prove to be satisfactory, Sophie took on her everyday routine cheerfully. However, trouble seemed to follow Sophie to test her endurance. First of all, the sleeping arrangements in the bungalow were not the best. There was only one small bedroom that Sophie occupied. A bed was set up in the living room and Ben would sleep with one of the boys, usually Sammy. Buddy slept on the couch. The girls, Mary, Rose, and Lena slept on the screened-in back porch.

On hot summer nights, Bud would even sleep on the flat roof over the porch for the lovely breezes that would flow from the Colorado River that was about two hundred yards away.

One night, a terrible thunderstorm swept through Austin. Trees swayed and dipped over, streets were flooded and rain drenched the bungalow on Brett Lane. The girls huddled together under a blanket that soon became soaked. Ben and Sophie had no idea the screened porch leaked.

Another night, the electrical wiring scared them half to death as a series of sparks were generated from the outlets throughout the house. It was becoming increasingly expensive for repairs and Ben and Sophie were aware that another move would have to be made, but several years passed before they were able to find a suitable house that was affordable. In the meantime, the girls had to endure the porch for a bedroom, while Sophie and Ben did the best they could on his small salary.

One bright and sunny afternoon in 1936, a favorite Aunt Sophie and her son, Dominic, arrived from Pennsylvania. While visiting with Sophie and Ben, she became impressed with Buddy, who was around eleven years old at the time, and asked if she could take him home with her to meet her boys, some of which were around Buddy's age. Sophie and Ben agreed thinking she and Dominic would bring him back in the fall for school.

But, Buddy's visit, which was supposed to be a summer

vacation, turned into a nine-month leave of absence. Finally, Ben had Sophie write to the aunt requesting his return. Aunt Sophie, it seems, was extremely religious, and so impressed with Buddy that she decided to steer him towards the priesthood. Buddy, on the other hand, wanted desperately to return home.

So, after much correspondence between Sophie and the aunt, Ben decided to take matters into his own hands, and sent the amount needed for a ticket. Without any further ado, Buddy was put on a train. These extra expenses were hard on the family budget, but somehow, they managed to get enough together for the ticket. Ben probably put in extra time at the bakery.

Buddy was ecstatic when the ticket arrived in Pennsylvania. He gave up the small paper route he had while there and counted the days until he was on his way back home.

Buddy's Aunt Sophie lived in Summerset County, Pennsylvania, south of Johnstown. In order to take the train back to Austin, Buddy's cousin, Dominic and his Aunt Sophie, had to drive him to Pittsburgh. Arrangements were then made with the train station people for Bud to be attended from Pittsburgh to St. Louis by a schoolteacher on her way to Terre Haute, Indiana.

He enjoyed her company immensely because "she was a constant source of information," and it helped to speed up the twelve-hour ride from Pittsburgh to St. Louis. However, the ride from St. Louis to Austin, was another story. He had lost the company of the schoolteacher and was totally on his own for fifteen more hours. Needless to say, Bud was glad to get home.

Interestingly, the schoolteacher wrote Bud after he returned home, and he in turn, sent her some lovely handkerchiefs. They corresponded for quite a long time.

Sophie and Ben's children were becoming adults, in spite of the cramped quarters on Brett Lane. They had all attended St. Mary's Parochial School up to the seventh grade. The girls, then, transferred to St. Mary's Academy, which was a junior high and high school. Low-income Catholic families were not required to pay tuition at that time. Sometimes, the nuns would assign jobs to those not paying to justify their everyday presence.

Since school was such a struggle for Sammy, he decided not to continue and found a job as an usher in a movie theater. Some time later, Steck, a bookbinding company, which is now known as Hart Graphics, hired him. Sammy also served his country in the Korean War, which ran from 1950 to 1953. He returned to Steck after the war as the company's truck driver until he retired.

Buddy, on the other hand, wanted to continue his education; it had always been his desire to attend St. Edward's University, which was a high school with a two-year junior college curriculum. But Ben had different ideas about his education. He felt Buddy didn't need any more education. He was working at the bakery after school, and could advance himself there after a period of time, but Buddy objected strongly.

"This is not what I want to do, Daddy," Bud said. Actually, the highlight of the bakery job to Bud was to go with the workers at five o'clock in the morning to the restaurant on Sixth and Red River, where he would scan the newspaper to see if Joe Di Maggio had extended his hitting streak. However, Bud had no intention of building a career working in the bakery.

Ben, being a fair man, agreed to accompany Buddy to St. Edward's.

"You will never get him in there without paying tuition," said Sophie.

Ben answered Sophie's remark by saying, "You don't know everything, Sophie. We will go tomorrow and we will see."

The principal at St. Edward's, to Sophie's astonishment, agreed to let Buddy attend tuition free. However, it was only meant to be an enticement, because after the first semester, a note was sent home informing Sophie and Ben, tuition would be required for the second semester. Buddy quit St. Edward's and enrolled in a public junior high for a half year. His final years from 9th to 12th grades were spent at Austin High School and working as a waiter at Victor's restaurant after school and on weekends.

His sister, Rose, joined him later and together they waited on tables. Bud feels that this was an enjoyable time of their life. Working for Victor prepared them for the easy personal one-on-one contact that came with meeting people, simply by following Victor's easy and friendly approach that he naturally had with all who met him.

It was during his stint at Austin High School that he met C. E. Williams, otherwise known as Jack Williams, who's parents owned the Red and White Grocery Store on Twelfth and Chicon Streets, where people came from all parts of

Austin to buy their famous "Peanut Patties." Jack and Buddy are still good friends today.

In February of 1951, Sophie and Ben's last daughter, Lena, was enjoying her junior year at St. Mary's Academy to the fullest. Being a very pretty teenager and cheerleader, she was selected the girl most popular with the St. Edward's High School students. The two schools joined together in many events and each year St. Edward's students selected their Campus Sweetheart. The class voted for Lena to reign as Queen for the coming year.

Needless to say, this event created a great deal of merriment in Sophie's household. To this day, Sophie has the article showing Lena's picture on the front page of "The Echo," St. Edward's school paper.

Chapter 14

Pearl Harbor, War and David

Ben, Sophie, Buddy and Lena were in the old Ford driving on South Congress Avenue when the news came over the radio. The Japanese had bombed Pearl Harbor. America was at war. Shock, worry and fear came into their minds and hearts, and Sophie's thoughts immediately centered on her brother, Joe, who had joined the Army a few months ago. Nofria had just recently written to her about Joe's enlistment.

American faces were saddened and strained as they went about their daily activities. They hadn't thought about or even considered "war" for a long time. President Roosevelt called it "a day of infamy." Many of us will never forget it!

The war began in December 1941, and Buddy became eighteen in March of 1943. He could think of nothing other than joining the Navy. He kept a calendar handy, crossing off the days until he was eighteen; and then it finally came. His draft notice arrived asking him to report the next morning. Excitedly, he went down to the recruiting office and after being physically examined, was rejected because of falling arches. He was devastated! However, a strange turn of events changed this outcome and his determination paid off several months later.

Through friends and stalwart efforts on his part, he was

referred to an Army General in the Norway Building on West 8th Street. During the interview, Buddy told the General about wanting to get into the Navy, and also how he had been rejected because of what he felt was a minor disability. He had never had any trouble with his feet and had walked for miles delivering newspapers as a youngster. However, the General found a different slant to Bud's request.

"You're Italian, aren't you?" he asked.

Bud nodded yes.

"I guess it would be nice to get free passage to your homeland, eh? You know, as a soldier, you could wind up in Italy."

Bud was shocked. This guy was implying that he had an ulterior motive to joining the service, and just wanted to go back to the old country. Bud stood up and said quietly. "I think you have the wrong idea, Sir. I want to serve in the military for the United States, which *is* my country."

As Bud turned to leave, the General said, "Just a minute, young man." He handed Bud a signed note and said, "Report to the office in the morning and good luck!"

On his way to the recruiting office the next morning, Bud ran into his friend, Art. "Where are you going, Buddy?"

"I'm on my way to a naval recruiting office. This time I think I'll make it," Bud replied.

"Well, I guess we can do this together, because that's where I'm going too! Only thing, Bud, I want the Marine Corps," Art said.

After Bud showed the note from the General and Art passed his physical examination, both were sent for induction at the Sam Houston Air Force Base.

Art was called first to submit his papers of introduction and medical acceptance to the sergeant at the desk. After careful scrutiny of Art's credentials, the sergeant said, "Something's wrong here. Your papers are out of order. Go back home until we get this situation straightened out. We will contact you."

Art said goodbye to Bud and left disappointed.

After he left, the sergeant began to quietly converse with someone at the next desk, and then said. "We need another volunteer to meet our quota for today. Anyone here interested?"

Bud stood up. He approached the desk, handed over his papers with the General's note attached, and was inducted into the Marine Corps on June 26, 1944. His excitement was overwhelming as he packed for San Diego to start boot camp.

After completing eight weeks of boot camp, Bud was on his way to Austin for a week's leave before returning for what was called "line camp." While playing cards on the train with some of his Marine buddies, they noticed a great deal of excitement taking place in the vestibule passage area between the cars of the train. Emerging from a swarm of Marines in close pursuit was this lovely young lady, curvaceously built, with long brown hair, who turned out to be none other than Buddy's sister, Mary.

After leaving St. Mary's Academy, Mary got a job as a dentist's receptionist, and through the years dated, and then married a young man who was now in the service. She was on her way home from visiting him in San Francisco and, quite coincidentally, happened to be on the same train as Buddy. It had been some time since they had seen one another.

As she came closer to where Buddy was sitting, he looked up and yelled, "Mary!"

With a quick turn of her head, Mary beamed and shouted, "BUDDY!" and they hugged.

You should have seen the faces on those Marines. Without hesitation, Buddy turned to the Marines and said, "In case you don't know it, this is my sister, Mary. She doesn't mind conversation, and even a harmless escort, *but* pawing is out!"

The rest of the trip went without incident, but not without the catcalls and whistles that erupted every so often as Mary and Buddy visited.

Sophie's girls, indeed, had her beauty and young men were attracted to them. Rose, petite and pretty met her young man at a St. Edward's dance. He was studying engineering and was due to graduate presently.

With mostly grownups in their household now, Sophie and Ben did not give any further thought to having more children. So, when Sophie began to get nauseated in the morning and bouts of sleepiness would come over her early afternoon, pregnancy never entered her mind. She decided it was a flu thing, and hoped it would go away.

It didn't!

Her period was late, but she began to think that perhaps she was entering menopause. Finally, Ben persuaded her to see the doctor and he confirmed that Sophie was pregnant.

Sophie seemed pleased with the news, but Ben was not sure of his feelings. He was close to fifty years old. "I'm too old to be a papa to another child," he told Sophie.

"Nonsense," answered Sophie. "We will do just fine and your age will not matter one bit." Sophie's nine months went smoothly and her delivery was easy. She smiled when the nurse handed her a beautiful little boy with a full head of black hair. Sophie passed him to Ben and his heart swelled as he looked down at his tiny little son. He was a replica of his mother.

"He's a pretty boy, Sophie. Stay home and take care of him. Okay?" Ben said..

"Okay, Ben," said Sophie. They called him David.

Chapter 15

Our Pledge of Allegiance

The contentment of their new surroundings had brought peace to the Nardecchia family, but there was no peace in the world. The war still continued. It was 1945, and Sophie's thoughts of patriotism were no different than other Americans. She had many desires and one was to become an American citizen. So, with some prodding, she talked Ben into going to the immigration service one morning to inquire about becoming United States citizens. They were required to fill out a short form, which Sophie helped Ben do. Then, they were handed a book to study and told to report back in one month for an exam.

Every evening after David was put to bed, Sophie and Ben would attempt studying. It was difficult for Ben. The questions were beyond his comprehension, and eventually Sophie's patience would run short and an argument would ensue. Sadly, Ben became discouraged and quit studying. He never became an American citizen. Sophie, on the other hand, excitedly looked forward to the day. She was told to be at the immigration service at ten o'clock in the morning. She had studied diligently the night before and felt confident.

"You should be coming with me, Ben," she said as she ran around getting dressed. "Wait a minute, I just happened to think. Why don't you come with me? You can sit in the seats behind and watch. What do you think?"

At first, Ben declined. Then he said, "Yeah, I come too. You be too nervous to go by yourself. I drive you." Sophie would have had to take the bus. It was many years later that she learned how to drive.

As they entered the courtroom, Ben took a seat toward the back of the room. Sophie was directed to the front to sit with the other candidates. There were six women and four men applying for citizenship. After all were seated, the bailiff called for order in the courtroom and the judge appeared. Sophie's knees were shaking. The judge gave a short speech, congratulating them on their perseverance and determination to be citizens of our great country; then, asked them all to come up to the bench.

He asked each participant a different question from the book they were asked to study. After they answered correctly, they were directed to stand before the American flag and place their right hand over their heart.

"You will all now recite the Pledge of Allegiance," said the judge. Sophie was so proud that she recited loud and clear. Ben could hear her all the way in back where he was sitting. She glanced back in his direction and saw him standing with his hand on his heart, trying desperately to repeat the words. On their way home, Sophie said, "Ben, in God's eyes, you became an American citizen also today."

A short time later, another letter arrived from Nofria. It had news about her brother Joe. It simply said, "We have received a notice that Joe is missing in action. We will let you know more in time."

With blinding tears in her eyes, Sophie took David and the letter over to her neighbor. "Sophie, there is still hope. Pray hard," was all her neighbor could offer at this time.

However, five months later another letter arrived from Nofria and this time it said, "Joe's body was found in a barn in Normandy. They are shipping him home for burial." Sophie sat down, put her head in her hands and sobbed. In telling her story, she could only say, "He was such a beautiful man."

Chapter 16

Lake Austin Boulevard

The enjoyment that came with raising David was far more than Sophie and Ben expected. The other members of the family still living at home found a tremendous amount of pleasure in watching him grow. However, their living situation at Brett Lane was getting worse. Cramped quarters persisted, constant repairs continued and expenses were out of line.

One day Rose said to Sophie, "Mom, I would like to have someone special over for dinner, but not here. Mary and Lena agree with me. There is a vacant house on Lake Austin Boulevard that really looks good. Would you take a look at it?"

Rose felt it would be a great improvement over the house they were living in now. There was a need to upgrade.

Sophie agreed to look, and the next morning the two made a special trip to Lake Austin to see a single family home that had just been vacated. The house was in a lovely residential location with walking distance to Deep Eddy, a swimming pool well known to most Austinites. There were large, lovely oak trees and a long walk up to the porch, which Sophie liked. However, the spray of bluebonnets surrounding the walkway was what really caught Sophie's eye, and she was sold completely. She hoped that the interior of the house was as pleasant as the exterior.

And it was. The front door opened into the parlor, with a bedroom on the right. The parlor arched into a small hall with a bathroom on the left and another bedroom on the right. The hall led directly into the kitchen, with a third bedroom on the right. It satisfied both Sophie and Rose entirely. However, Sophie wondered how Ben would feel about another move. A bit of strategy would have to be used to get him to consider moving again.

That evening Sophie told Ben about their visit to Lake Austin Blvd. At first Ben was reluctant. However, as they talked she pointed out the constant electrical problems, the plumbing hazards and the fact that another child living there made them even more crowded than before.

Also, Sophie discovered through a reliable source that back taxes were owed on the property. After the University was notified, they agreed to pay the property taxes, but because Sophie and Ben lived on the property, they were accountable for the interest accumulated, which amounted to a couple of hundred dollars. When Ben heard this bit of news, he agreed to accompany Rose and Sophie to look at the house on Lake Austin. Rose had a permanent job at the time, so she helped Ben and Sophie get the amount requested together, and the family left Brett Lane.

They loved their new home and the working members agreed to help with the mortgage payments and contribute to its upkeep. Sophie was thrilled with the big backyard and worked on her vegetable garden at every opportunity.

One morning, her neighbor leaned over the fence and

said, "Good morning."

Sophie nonchalantly said, "Morning." She didn't even look up. Sophie took her time becoming too friendly with neighbors now. She knew Ben didn't like aggressive neighbors, so she kept her response very casual.

"I'm Mrs. Becker and I see you're starting a garden. What are you going to grow?" asked Mrs. Becker.

"Vegetables," said Sophie. "I had a big vegetable garden where we lived before, and can't wait to see this one grow."

"Well, I believe in growing fresh vegetables myself," said Mrs. Becker.

With that comment, Sophie stopped working and looked up. She walked over to the fence and peeked over at Mrs. Becker's garden. Without a stretch of the imagination, this was the largest vegetable garden Sophie had ever seen.

"Come over any time you like," said Mrs. Becker. From that day forward their friendship grew and Mrs. Becker taught her everything she knew about organic and natural foods.

Sophie fell in love with natural foods, spreading the word to every person she met. She learned about raw sugar, unbleached flour, and the dangers of preservatives, composts and even fresh milk. She and Ben would travel miles to Dunbar's farm for milk right out of the cow twice a week, and grocery store fruits sprayed with pesticides were totally unacceptable. She also learned about the Whole Food Store's organic produce department from Mrs. Becker, and never again shopped at another grocery store.

Not only did she become obsessed with natural foods; she embraced completely the practice of natural living. She would scold people who smoked and forbade it vehemently in her presence. She and Ben had many arguments because she insisted he smoke outdoors. Their clothing was laundered in Ivory flakes and bleach was out of the question. She would scrub stains out on a scrubbing board leaning over a bathtub. Never in her entire life did she own a dryer or want one. In fact, Sophie won a dryer one year and sold it.

She still hangs her clothes on a line outdoors for *that hot sun out there*. Sophie has a washing machine now, but uses it for large items only, such as, sheets, blankets, etc. She continues to scrub most of her wearing apparel over the bathtub on a scrubbing board.

As the years went on, Sophie became extreme. She juiced her own carrots, cleaned her house only in vinegar and warm water and swallowed vitamins by the bottles. She became paranoid over germs and would not allow anyone in her house with a cold. She began to collect everything that could be recycled. Magazines, newspapers, plastic bags, coffee cans; you name it, Sophie kept it. There was never a spot at the kitchen table to place a plate for eating, or a path to walk through her house because of the debris she had collected. She could have been called a fanatic or she may just have been ahead of her time!

Sophie never had colds or suffered bouts of the flu. Her energy level was boundless, starting her day at five-thirty every morning and continuing on until seven-thirty each night. When she finally sat down, neither her fingers nor mind relaxed. She would crochet or read anything and everything not only once but several times.

Sophie and Ben shared their sorrows and their joys. On this particular day, the joy was overwhelming. Radios blasted the news, schools closed, companies sent employees home, ticker tape parades flooded the nation, and Americans wept. The war was over. Germany was defeated and Hitler annihilated. Franklin Delano Roosevelt had died and, now President Harry S. Truman ordered the nuclear bomb to be dropped on Japan, a decision that brought the war to an end but has fueled the fires for critics of today.

World War II ended. The best part was that our sons, lovers, husbands and friends would come home again. This time prayer worked for Sophie. When the news broke, Buddy was on Iwo Jima, but unharmed.

When Buddy returned home, some changes had been made in the old homestead. Ben was no longer at the bakery, but worked as a custodian at a bar and eatery on Twelfth Street, which today is a popular Austin restaurant and tavern. The girls were all married and having children of their own, Sammy was contemplating marriage with a girl he had known for some time.

Chapter 17

Changes

As Nofria and Sophie corresponded, Sophie began to suspect desperation whenever Nofria mentioned Salvatore. She would write things like, "Your father seems quieter than usual, or, he has those old indigestion problems again. I told him to cut back on the amount he eats." The last letter, she wrote," Your father still complains about chest pains, but refuses to see a doctor. He is taking Joe's death hard."

Sophie wanted badly to see her family again, especially Salvatore. He was always so special to her, but David was simply too young to leave and financially, they could not afford a trip to New Jersey. So, she wrote as often as she could and somehow began to establish a bond between her and Nofria.

Then, a tragic accident happened. Salvatore was running to catch a bus early one morning in New Jersey, when he had a heart attack, and fell face down in a snow embankment. He was dead by the time the ambulance reached the hospital. It was 1947, and he was sixty-one years old After passing this news on to Sophie, Nofria stopped writing for a long time. Sophie was completely heartbroken.

Sophie was again getting the itch to go back to work and scouting around for someone to take care of David. But, to her disappointment, Ben said "no" when Sophie mentioned returning to work.

"David too young. He needs his mamma. Stay home, Sophie."

So Sophie waited until David was in school full time before considering the working world again. She had heard that St. Mary's School was looking for another employee to work in their kitchens. She applied and was hired. But again, this was not a good decision. She was assigned to washing dishes and loading the dishwasher that brought her many problems she did not anticipate. Her hands again began to suffer from boiling hot water, so after one year, Sophie quit.

However, some time later, a friend told her about Austin High School looking for a cashier to work in the cafeteria. She was hired and found this a happy working experience that made her feel worthwhile again. It was also great having the extra money. Ben had bought a used 1934 Ford, and he and Buddy kept it running. Sophie had wanted a new refrigerator and washing machine, and to her delight, this became a reality with the extra money coming into their home. For a change, life was sweeter.

Sophie's opportunity to visit New Jersey and see her family again came in June of 1957. Buddy was living in Chicago at the time. He had been hired by a gas company there through a friend's recommendation, and married a Chicago girl.

Rose was now married to her St. Edward's graduate and had two boys. She and her family planned a trip to visit Buddy, and then continue on to New Jersey to visit Sophie's family. Sophie and Ben agreed to take David and joined them. These were pleasant memories for Sophie and she reflects on the time spent there as being very special. She not only visited with her mother, but her brother, Nick, and her two sisters, Mary and Augie.

Sophie made one more trip to New Jersey in 1968 two years after Ben died. This time it was with Buddy and his family. She was sixty years old. Nofria was seventy-eight. Both were in prime health. It was the last time Sophie saw her mother. They continued to write letters, but eventually, Nofria went into a nursing home and remained there until she died at ninety-six. Sophie had another sister, Angelina, who lived in Monroe, Michigan. In her early fifties, she was driving home one day, and in an attempt to get across a railroad track as a train approached, she didn't quite clear the tracks when the train caught the back of her car. She was thrown from the car and killed instantly.

At the present time, three of Salvatore and Nofria's nine children remain, Sophie, Nick and Mary. Nick and his wife still live in New Jersey and Mary is in a nursing home.

In August of 1966, Sophie was still working at Austin High School and David was in San Diego, California, completing a stint with the Navy. Ben had retired from his custodial job and was working part-time at Victor's Restaurant on the University Drag.

A letter arrived from Nofria saying she and her granddaughter would be coming to Austin by train and she stated the date and time. Sophie and Ben were both surprised and excited. They picked them up at the train station and entertained them in a wonderful Italian fashion. Visitors were always taken to Victor's for good food, and Nofria was no exception. When Nofria and her granddaughter left, Sophie had a peaceful and satisfied feeling about their visit. But, the peace she felt did not last long.

Exactly two weeks later, Ben punched out at the restaurant, said good-bye to the cashier and started for the door. As he opened the door, he heard a sound that was very close to a gunshot. He listened again, but it was gone, so he dismissed it as perhaps a car backfiring.

Then, he saw people running and not just running, but running scared. Then, another shot. He grabbed hold of a young boy running past him, and said, "What is going on?

"Some nut is on top of the UT Tower, killing people!" The young man said.

The Tower sits on the University Campus and is about a block and a half from the restaurant.

Ben walked the distance to where he could see the Tower, leaving his car in the parking lot of the restaurant, to see what was going on. When he arrived, police were pushing people into doorways for protection against the bullets raining down on the campus from the Tower. He heard screaming all around him. It was then that he saw people on the ground. They were not moving. Somehow, Ben managed to get away from the scene. He ran back to his car and drove home. This whole episode affected him badly. When Sophie got home from work, he was sitting on the front porch, perspiring profusely. He ate very little supper that night; he just sat and watched the event on television.

Charles Whitman was a disturbed young man who had attended the University of Texas in 1961. Because of low grades and other prominent problems, he left the University and went into the service. While in the service, he attended East Carolina State College and was discharged in 1964. Because his academic ability had improved, Whitman was allowed to re-enter the University of Texas. However, his parents' divorce and other family situations became terribly stressful for him, and he sought medical and psychiatric advice at the University Health Center; but he failed to return as directed for further assistance.

During the pre-dawn hours of August 1, 1966, Whitman killed his mother and wife. Then, bought a variety of ammunition and a shotgun; went to the University Tower, up to the twenty-eighth floor, killed two people and wounded two others as he ascended the stairs. When he arrived at the observation deck, he opened fire on people crossing the campus and on nearby streets. Altogether, sixteen people were killed and thirty were wounded before the police were able to corner and kill him on the observation deck. It is still considered one of the worst mass murders in modern United States history.

Ben had witnessed enough of the event to create a physical and mental effect on him. As they watched television the night of the event, he said to Sophie, "See the policeman by that store front? That's where I was standing." Ben was a man of a few words, but Sophie could detect a disturbance in his voice while he talked. That night in bed he tossed and turned and Sophie worried about him.

The next morning, Ben arose and dressed. As he started out the door, Sophie yelled from the kitchen, "Where are you going?"

Ben turned and said something, but she didn't hear him.

So, she left what she was doing in the kitchen and walked into the living room.

"Where?" she asked.

"To Capitol Chevrolet," he replied briskly.

"But, you said your car wasn't running too good. How are you getting there?" asked Sophie.

"Walking," Ben shouted.

He had told Sophie the night before, he needed a part for the car and could install it himself, but she never expected him to walk. The car dealership was at least two miles from where they lived, not to mention that the temperature was already about eighty degrees at nine o'clock in the morning. She threw her hands up in exasperation and went back to the kitchen.

Sophie was sitting in Ben's chair, watching the aftershock on television of the shootings that took place the day before, when Ben walked in the door. The temperature had reached well into the nineties and Ben looked like he had been put through a wringer. He was perspiring heavily; his shirt was soaking wet and his face was flushed.

Sophie began her usual reprimanding, and so he went out on the front porch and sat down.

He sat about five minutes, came back into the house, and said to Sophie, "Looks like it's going to rain," and went into the bathroom.

It was there, it happened. Ben fell over. Sophie heard the thud, and went running. Those were the last words that he spoke.

She became hysterical, not knowing what to do. She held his head in her hands, screaming, "Ben, Ben speak to me. No!

No! Don't go! Don't leave me!" She laid his head down and ran to the telephone. She was so upset, she could not think of who to call. Suddenly, her neighbor, Mrs. Becker, came to her mind and she dialed her number.

Mrs. Becker answered the phone. She heard Sophie screaming, "It's Ben! It's Ben! Please come!"

After reaching Mrs. Becker, Sophie released the phone, letting it dangle against the wall in the kitchen, and ran back to Ben.

Mrs. Becker called for an ambulance, but she could see Ben had taken his last breath. The doctors agreed at the hospital that Ben had died of a massive heart attack. Sophie's Ben was gone.

As I sat with Sophie in her living room, hearing the end of their life together, it occurred to me that it was a beautiful life.   He was strong and she was brave always ready to take on any or all the blows life sent them. Over a course of fifty years, love was shown here between these two people, more than most could realize. Struggling to level the peaks and valleys of every day is love.

Sophie reached for the towel hanging over the back of her chair and wiped her eyes as she looked at me and then at Ben's picture.

Sophie had her moments of grief after Ben's death. Funeral arrangements were made with the help of her children who lived nearby, but the nights alone after Ben's burial were unbearable. To get past the worse period, she stayed at Sammy's home for a while, but that didn't seem to help.

She returned home and decided she was not about to succumb to the sorrows of life, and again, climbed her way up out of the depths of depression. She respected and observed her mourning period for a year, and then began to strengthen her courage once more.

After repeated walks to the grocery store and to work, she realized that she needed a better means of transportation. She was tired of getting caught in the rain and the heat. Her neighbor and friend, who was a mechanic, suggested she learn how to drive. The encouragement was what she needed and so she took driving lessons, and with his help, purchased a 1968 Dodge Dart. She still has that car today. While arranging and re-arranging this new life that had suddenly come to her, she received a phone call informing her that the City of Austin was buying up right-of-way space for a highway to be called Mo-Pac.

Sophie's home, as well as, many others on Lake Austin Blvd. was in the North-South corridor of the highway planned, and she would have to move. The City would give her the fair market value of her home.

Almost immediately, she called a Realtor and began to look at homes. For days and weeks she looked at one house after another without any luck. She knew what she wanted and began to think it was not out there. Then, her Realtor said one afternoon; "I have one more home to show you today, if you're not too tired."

"Oh, all right," Sophie said. "Although, one more is about all I can take."

The minute she walked in the door, she knew it was the one. After looking it all over, she knew in her heart that this was what she wanted. She has been on Margaret Street now for twenty-five years and still loves it.

One interesting fact that Sophie mentioned is worth inserting here. A policeman owned the house that Sophie moved into on Margaret Street. Right next door lived another policeman, who happened to be the officer who shot and killed Charles Whitman on the day he terrorized the University of Texas.

Between the time of Ben's death and Sophie's move, David returned from the Navy. He was a handsome young man in his twenties. He lived with Sophie until he met and married a young lady. They had two children and Sophie spent a good deal of her time taking care of the children. They were special to her, but sadly, the marriage did not last. He returned home until he accepted a welding job, which eventually took him to Arkansas. After David's divorce, he met and married again in Arkansas and lives there today.

With David gone and his children coming over infrequently, Sophie began to look for companionship. A friend and neighbor encouraged her to attend the Senior Citizen dances. And, since she had her car to come and go, she thought, "Why not!" Besides, she had always wanted to learn how to dance.

Bravely, she dressed up one evening and went to the Senior Citizen Activity Center near, or close, to Oltorf. Sophie at this point was sixty or sixty-one. It appeared to her that the people she met at the Center were much older, but she was determined to learn how to dance and stayed on course when the music started.

Bill Church was the music director. Whether he spotted her or she him is not definite at this point, but they connected and began to dance. If you recall, earlier in the story, the happiest time of Sophie's life after leaving the cotton fields was when she and Ben would dance to the phonograph music. Well, here she was again enjoying the sublime rhythm of the music and swaying on a dance floor. She was mesmerized!

And, Bill Church was captivated with her charm. Sophie is petite, pretty and very sweet. She continued to return to the Senior Center and Bill continued to dance with her every week. In fact, he was supposed to be the dance instructor, but it was obvious, that Sophie was his favorite student. They began to date and Bill did not only teach her how to dance, but how to have fun and enjoy life. He was a totally different man than Ben, and she loved the difference.

Bill and Sophie were married September 1982, but sadly, the marriage had problems. Bill had been a carpenter by trade, and after he moved into Sophie's house, he wanted to make one improvement after another. She allowed a few things, but when he started talking about knocking down walls and remodeling the whole house, it was time for her to say "No." Bill was crushed.

During the course of their marriage, they separated, divorced, reunited, separated and divorced again, until finally, Bill moved to an assisted living home. He remained there until his death in 1993.

Afterword

Sophie lives alone and wants it that way. Mary and Rose live in Texas, but not close by. Lena is in Pennsylvania and David lives in Arkansas. Actually, Sammy and Buddy live the closest to her. Buddy and his wife moved from Chicago to Austin a few years ago, and now reside in Georgetown, Texas.

Buddy keeps a watchful eye on her, and the others visit from time to time. She has twenty grandchildren and numerous great-grandchildren. They visit occasionally.

The family will organize and arrange reunions from time to time. However, she prefers to stay home. She is accustomed to her surroundings, and does not desire to travel anymore.

"I have been to Chicago, California, and Arkansas. I traveled a lot when I was younger," Sophie will say. Now, I just want to stay home."

Shortly after Bud and his wife moved to Austin, Texas, Sophie fell and was hospitalized for a few days. She was disoriented and confused so her doctor prescribed medication and recommended a short stint in St. David's Pavilion, which is a Senior Citizen Rehab Center where she would have close supervision.

This was not a happy time for her and she wrote the following, signaling just how depressed she was living in the

Center.

"One day when I went down the line for dinner, I saw some muffins on the counter. I asked what kind they were. She said bran muffins. That bran muffin was no more a muffin than I was. It was so sweet and no bran in it. I couldn't eat it. Corn bread was the same, so sweet and crumbly -- Mother Sophie"

She remained ten days in the Pavilion and has vowed never again to return.

From that day on, she arranged her life in a convenient manner for her; doing the things she could handle and seeking out others to help her with the things she couldn't.

She has a special friend who shops and delivers her groceries, and she shares one or two days a week with her son, Buddy and his wife. They also bring her an assortment of meals once a week to be sure she eats properly, and makes sure her doctor appointments and medications are up to date. Sophie also hired a cleaning lady to help with her laundry and chores around the house.

At ninety-two years old, Sophie maintains her financial affairs, writes her own letters, cooks her own meals occasionally, and faithfully every morning eagerly works out in her backyard. She is quite amazing!

As I sat and documented her story, I also sat and read it to her when it was finished. She smiled and said, "It is just a life, everybody has one."

To order additional copies of *Sophie and Ben*

Name _____

Address _____

_____

$12.95 x _____ copies =   _____

Sales Tax
(Texas residents add 7.25% sales tax)   _____

Please add $3.50 postage and handling per book   _____

Total amount due: _____

Please send check or money order for books to:

Word Wright International
P.O. Box 1785
Georgetown, TX 78627

Please make checks payable to:

Helen Nardecchia

Printed in the United States
1475600005B/370-468

9 780970 061560